DE QUINCEY'S CONSECRATION
OF ROMANTICISM

ANDREW KEANIE

Greenwich Exchange
London

Greenwich Exchange, London

First published in Great Britain in 2020
All rights reserved

Andrew Keanie © 2020

Printed and bound by imprintdigital.com
Cover design by December Publications
Tel: 07951511275

Greenwich Exchange Website: www.greenex.co.uk

Cataloguing in Publication Data is available from the British Library

Cover art: Thomas De Quincey by Sir John Watson Gordon
(reproduced courtesy of the National Galleries of Scotland)

ISBN: 978-1-910996-32-4

To Eleanor and Emma

CONTENTS

Introduction ♦ De Quincey's Consecration of Romanticism

> A man left alone in the universe would have no rights whatsoever, but he would have obligations.
>
> – Simone Weil, *The Need for Roots*

The artists and intellectuals of the middle ages knew not our hypocrisies. This is not to say that they were ignorant of our ineradicable immoralities. They knew how to hate them. They published them, sculpted them on cathedral portals and spread them in verses of poetry. They wanted to tear open the robes and reveal the man, making him ashamed of all the ugliness of his low animality. They did not want to let the brute wallow in and enjoy his vice; they wanted to put him on his knees and make him lift his head.

In autobiographical writing since the Middle Ages, acknowledgements – and even analyses – of base appetites as well as spiritual aspirations have brought to light some interesting examples of cognitive dissonance. There is no better chronicler of this mental discomfort than Thomas De Quincey, who was living in the gutter and looking at the stars decades before Oscar Wilde would make it proverbial. De Quincey was as much in the nightmare of his own delinquencies as Lord Byron. He understood as painfully and personally as Byron what it is to have a divided nature, half dust and half deity.

Intellectually, De Quincey felt on top of the world, the scholar-angel with dazzling recall and searching eloquence, able to make new patterns of connection and meaning for the general reader. He had, as he put it in *Suspiria de Profundis*, 'the higher faculty of an electric aptitude for seizing analogies, and by means of those aerial pontoons passing like lightning from one topic to another.' But morally, he often felt worm-eaten, maggot-ridden, and about to have his sins found out. He could usefully be thought of as a precursor to Oscar Wilde's Dorian Gray (with his wretched picture).

De Quincey was a character assassin 'with the venom of a wasp in his heart' (as Thomas Carlyle, stung by a review, complained), a user of alcohol, drugs and prostitutes, and a plagiarist. Mentally, he was so traumatised and disfigured (by the harm he did to others as well as to himself) that the iniquity seemed sometimes to shine out from within him despite his childlike demeanor and gentlemanly refinement. 'Eccovi, this Child has been in Hell!', said Carlyle.

By De Quincey's generation, confessional writing had already existed for a long time. It was already being recognised as falling short of actual contrition. Byron felt that Saint Augustine's 'fine Confessions ... make the reader envy his transgressions' (*Don Juan*,

I, 47), and as William Blake put it, Jean-Jacques Rousseau's *Confessions* 'throw the sand against the wind,/And the wind blows it back again.'

De Quincey's publication of *Confessions of an English Opium-Eater* (1821) was like the opening of a new eye on literature and life. The author seemed suddenly to have extended the province of what it was permissible to write autobiography about. He could take cognisance of, and criticise, previous confessional writings, but he could also point with knowledge and enthusiasm to the most exciting contemporary poets, William Wordsworth and Samuel Taylor Coleridge. In doing so, De Quincey led readers all the way into a whole new perspective. He brought about not the beginning but the consecration of a new kind of literature: Romanticism.

1 ♦ Romanticism: an English counterculture Taylor-Made

'It may seem wonderful,' said Thomas Taylor, the English Platonist, 'that language, which is the only method we have of conveying our conceptions, should at the same time be a hindrance to our advancement in philosophy: but the wonder ceases when we consider, that it is seldom studied as the vehicle of truth, but is too frequently esteemed for its own sake, independent of its connection with things.'

For Taylor, the greatest thinkers, such as Plato and Plotinus, 'studied things more than words', and 'Truth alone was the ultimate object of their search.' Taylor considered that 'he who wishes to emulate their glory, and participate their wisdom, will study their doctrines more than their language, and value the depth of their understandings far beyond the elegance of their composition.' (Thomas Taylor: *Collected Writings of Plotinus*, xiii)

Taylor influenced many English writers of his time such as Benjamin Bailey, William Blake, Lord Byron, Samuel Taylor Coleridge, Leigh Hunt, John Keats, Charles Lamb, Thomas Love Peacock, Percy Bysshe Shelley, Robert Southey and William Wordsworth.[1] (He also influenced the American transcendentalist writers such as Ralph Waldo Emerson, Henry Thoreau and Bronson Alcott.)

These writers tended to object to language being used in an outward and mechanical way at the expense of human emotions. Keats famously put it in these lines:

> Do not all charms fly
> At the mere touch of cold philosophy?
> There was an awful rainbow once in heaven:
> We know her woof, her texture; she is given
> In the dull catalogue of common things.
> Philosophy will clip an Angel's wings,
> Conquer all mysteries by rule and line,
> Empty the haunted air, and gnomed mine –
> Unweave a rainbow ...
>
> – Keats, *Lamia*

It wasn't just an exclusively *out*ward and mechanical mode of discourse that these writers wanted to avoid. *In*ward and

---

[1] 'Pagan Taylor: The Emergence of a Public Character 1785-1804. An Enquiry into the Life and Selected Works of Thomas Taylor the Platonist (1758-1835)' (PhD Thesis, University of York, 2006), Steven George Critchley, 330-31

mechanical was problematic too. According to one eminent child of the English Romantic revolution, Alfred Lord Tennyson, there seemed no way of knowing whether putting one's grief into words (in Tennyson's case, obsessively for seventeen years from 1833 to 1849) is 'right' or 'wrong'. It is 'sometimes' held 'half a sin' by Tennyson's speaker:

> I sometimes hold it half a sin
> To put in words the grief I feel
> For words, like Nature, half reveal
> Yet half conceal the soul within.
>
> — Tennyson, *In Memoriam*

The premise seems no sooner to have been thought than it has had to be hedged and qualified and elaborated, albeit all within the tight ABBA format. Tennyson sustained the approach, effectively constructing a 723-stanza-long panopticon in which, arguably, all the angels and demons of bereavement have been quartered and can be observed. Equally arguably though, 'the extraordinarily sumptuous, sheerly mellifluous noise' (Seamus Perry, *Tennyson*, 1) is of poetry making nothing happen:

> Still onward winds the dreary way;
> I with it; for I long to prove
> No lapse of moons can canker Love,
> Whatever fickle tongues may say.
>
> — *In Memoriam*

Tennyson had mixed feelings about recognising *In Memoriam* – which is about his slow coming to terms with the death of his close friend Arthur Hallam – as 'The sad mechanic exercise,/Like dull narcotics, numbing pain.' Writing on and on about one's own feelings without connection to the changing circumstances of the external world is maybe just as futile as touching those circumstances with cold philosophy. In the final balance of such things, who is to say?

Hypersensitive though he was to their ambiguity and entropy, Tennyson nevertheless needed – as of course all writers need – words. He reached for them not just to attempt to define a state of mind, but also for a sort of warmth. But even as he did so he worried that his readers would form but a vague sense of his soul in agony:

> In words, like weeds, I'll wrap me o'er,
> Like coarsest clothes against the cold;
> But that large grief which these enfold
> Is given in outline and no more.

> – *In Memoriam*

These words have been written by a poet who knows that equivocation is the inevitable outcome of investigating 'the mystery underlying the processes' (John Beer, *Coleridge's Play of Mind*, 240) of life. He knows that words don't just reveal and conceal the truth – they *half* reveal and *half* conceal it. Even if he speaks by the card, equivocation may still undo him. If he is too logical, the mystery may remain hidden. 'There are more things in heaven and earth, Horatio,/Than are dreamt of in your philosophy' (*Hamlet*, I, 5). If he is too lyrical, readers may be left with mere mumbo jumbo, or a sort of somnambular mumbling or muttering unfit for open court – little more to go on than a half-soothing, half-solacing, half-laughable experience of, say, Coleridge's 'damsel with a dulcimer/In a vision once I saw', or Lewis Carroll's 'Jabberwock, with eyes of flame' that 'Came whiffling through the tulgey wood,/And burbled as it came'.

Words might help one build a shelter from life's terrible energies, or a system in which to lock oneself and preach from within at one's ease. But that shelter or system will only be temporary. As Charles Baudelaire put it, 'a system is a kind of damnation; it is always necessary to be inventing a new one, and the drudgery involved is a cruel punishment.' Baudelaire is keenly sensible that his means are finite and his needs infinite. He might at one point in his life put into words a system that seems 'beautiful, spacious, vast, convenient, neat, and above all, water-tight'. But at a later point in his life the beauty will evaporate, the spaciousness will shrink, the convenience will become inconvenience, and above all, the water-tightness will be lost. This will happen because 'always some spontaneous, unexpected product of universal vitality' (*The Mirror of Art*, 194) will throw into ruin the false configuration. Baudelaire conveys something of how draughty and uncomfortable it feels — analogous perhaps with being half in and half out of the womb — to know that one's shelter, or system, is no longer providing the support it did at first, and that one must somehow thrust through it and leave it behind in search of something else.

Blake caught the emotional rawness of the predicament:

> Into the dangerous world I leapt,
> Helpless, naked, piping loud,
> Like a fiend hid in a cloud.
>
> — 'Infant Sorrow', *Songs of Experience*

Blake's speaker — or seeker — can only exert himself so much before becoming silent and resentful, as many do:

> Struggling in my father's hands,
> Striving against my swaddling bands,

> Bound and weary, I thought best
> To sulk upon my mother's breast.
>
> — 'Infant Sorrow', *Songs of Experience*

Tennyson traces the growth (or rather the rising self-involvement) of a soul from infancy, through the narrowing and sharpening of itself into the solitary confinement in which it must settle.

> The baby new to earth and sky,
>   What time his tender palm is prest
>   Against the circle of the breast,
> Has never thought that 'this is I.'
>
> But as he grows he gathers much,
>   And learns the use of 'I' and 'me,'
>   And finds 'I am not what I see,
> And other than the things I touch.
>
> So rounds he to a separate mind
>   From whence clear memory may begin,
>   As thro' the frame that binds him in
> His isolation grows defined.
>
> — *In Memoriam*

Wordsworth had already put it in a memorable nutshell in his 'Ode: Intimations of Immortality from Recollections of Early Childhood':

> Heaven lies about us in our infancy!
> Shades of the prison-house begin to close
>   Upon the growing Boy ...

Baudelaire would become an exuberant expression of that

prisoner, as well as of Tennyson's individual defined in his isolation, and of Blake's fiend that was once hid in a cloud but is now clarified in angry repose. He did not ask to be born. He has been born all the same. He finds himself ever-agitated by appetites, curiosities and yearnings. He is incurably restless, yet he must force himself to still that restlessness because, inexorably and infuriatingly, all life's energies (including the energies of restlessness) have to be husbanded.

But even in assuming the compulsory position of stilled restlessness, Baudelaire has managed to find some saving play of mind – if he must 'rest' his 'philosophic conscience' he will rest it facetiously: 'I took a great decision. To escape from the horror ... I haughtily resigned myself to modesty ... I returned to seek refuge in impecable *naiveté*. I humbly beg pardon of the academics of all kinds who occupy the various workrooms of our artistic factory. But it is *there* that my philosophic conscience has found its rest.' (*The Mirror of Art*, 194)

Having found himself driven out of his artificial paradise, he has garlanded himself with the artificial flowers of evil. He is an outsider in the sense that we all are, finding 'no end in wandering mazes lost' (as Coleridge put it, quoting Milton),[2] feeling isolated from wisdom, from Eden, from the One, from ourselves, and obliged, as Thomas Taylor put it, to 'pursue matter in its dark labyrinths' (*Collected Writings of Plotinus*, 2). Lost and living on our wits, we can only find ourselves oscillating on an arc of attitude between playfulness and warfare. Shelley too put our problem fiercely and memorably:

---

[2] In his *Biographia Literaria* (1817), Coleridge quotes from Milton's *Paradise Lost* (II, 559-61).

'Tis *we*, who lost in stormy visions, keep
With phantoms an unprofitable strife,
And in mad trance, strike with our spirit's knife
Invulnerable nothings. – *We* decay
Like corpses in a charnel; fear and grief
Convulse us and consume us day by day,
And cold hopes swarm like worms within our living clay.

– *Adonais*, XXXIX

And, again, as Baudelaire put it,

Like seething millions of intestinal worms,
A race of Demons riots in our brains

– *The Flowers of Evil*, 7

Like Milton's Satan in Heaven before his ejection from it, we were happy and safe once, whether as the growing foetus in the amniotic fluid or the growing boy in the nice family home. But sooner or later we had to leave and get stuck into the next problem in which we found ourselves. Having been brought up in such a loving family atmosphere, Victor Frankenstein – and all his dabbling among the unhallowed damps of the grave, and his disturbing of dead matter with profane fingers – reads the more compellingly in this context. Our arts (and sciences) are decidedly unhallowed when we merely engage our intellect with the operations of sense on the materials to hand.

The pattern in the countercultural carpet here is Thomas Taylor. 'With respect to true philosophy, you must be sensible that all modern sects are in a state of barbarous ignorance: for Materialism and its attendant Sensuality, have darkened the eyes of the *many*, with mists of error; and are continually strengthening their corporeal tie.' That there are matters in which reason cannot see at all takes an individual with strong spiritual defences to say. Taylor's uncompromising position seems to have been perceived by the Romantics as one they could take their bearings from:

> For the word philosophy, which implies the love of wisdom, is now become the ornament of folly. In the times of its inventor, and for many succeeding ages, it was expressive of modesty and worth; in our days, it is the badge of impudence and vain pretensions. It was formerly the symbol of the profound and contemplative genius; it is now the mark of the superficial and unthinking practitioner. It was once reverenced by kings, and clothed in the robes of nobility; it is now (according to its true acceptation) abandoned and despised, and ridiculed by the vilest Plebeian.
>
> – *Collected Writings of Plotinus*, 19

Blake not only said that the prevailing mode of discourse of his country comprised 'woven labyrinths ... snares & traps & wheels & pit-falls & dire mills' ('Jerusalem'). He also mounted an attack on it.

> Bring me my Bow of burning gold:
> Bring me my Arrows of desire:
> Bring me my Spear: O clouds unfold!
> Bring me my Chariot of fire!
>
> I will not cease from Mental Fight,
> Nor shall my sword sleep in my hand:
> Till we have built Jerusalem,
> In Englands green & pleasant Land.

Baudelaire (hating the world with his fire and ice), Taylor (hating 'the lucre of traffic and merchandize') and Shelley (hating the 'moral desert' in which he found himself) were all capable of attack very early on in their writing lives.

Wordsworth, however, is an interesting case. No verbal arsonist, and not inclined to the same vehemence of expression as the other writers inspired by Taylor, Wordsworth took a while to find his voice. But when he did, he would speak to the depths so resoundingly as to involve the roots of his own life with the roots of others' lives – including, crucially, Thomas De Quincey's.

2 ♦ Into the Depths: Romanticism and Wordsworth

> I was often unable to think of external things as having external existence, and I communed with all that I saw as something not apart from, but inherent in, my own immaterial nature. Many times while going to school have I grasped at a wall or tree to recall myself from the abyss of idealism to the reality. At that time I was afraid of such processes.
> – From Wordsworth's letter to Isabella Fenwick, 1843

Though the depths did open to him, they did not become articulable for Wordsworth right away. He suffered emotionally and evolved as a writer. Through experience of living and writing, he learned that it was not possible for him simply to have an experience (however intense) or visit a place (however magnificent) and then write deeply and meaningfully about it. His best poetry could only be written (as he would realise in his late twenties) when he had *re*visited an experience or place in imagination and memory.

One of his first sustained poetic efforts was *Descriptive Sketches*, which he wrote in 1790 at the age of twenty. Then (the time of Revolutionary France) he went on a walking tour of mainland

Europe (including France) with his friend Robert Jones (his fellow-student at Cambridge), and he saw sublime scenery, savage poverty and civil unrest. He (brought up an English Protestant) had a love affair in France with a Catholic, Annette Vallon, who would have their daughter, Caroline, in 1792.

It seems he was forced by the circumstances of war between England and France to leave his lover and daughter in a hurry to return to England. This was all in the couple of years just after the beginning of the French Revolution in 1789. (Wordsworth wrote *Descriptive Sketches* in 1791-92).

He saw, and indeed crossed on foot, the famous Alps, which had been written about already by, for example, Thomas Gray, who had said that if you did not believe in God, you would be instantly converted simply by seeing the Grand Chartreuse:

> Not a precipice, not a torrent, not a cliff, but is pregnant with religion and poetry. There are certain scenes that would awe an atheist into belief, without the help of other argument. One need not have a very fantastic imagination to see spirits there at noonday. You have death perpetually before your eyes, only so far removed, as to compose the mind without frightening it.
> – Thomas Gray's letter dated 16 November 1739, describing his journey to the Grande Chartreuse during his Continental tour.

Wordsworth went full of expectations. He expected much of the Alps and of himself as a poet. Here is an example of what he produced:

> 'Tis storm; and, hid in mist from hour to hour,
> All day the floods a deepening murmur pour;
> The sky is veiled, and every cheerful sight:
> Dark is the region as with coming night;

> But what a sudden burst of overpowering light!
> Triumphant on the bosom of the storm,
> Glances the fire-clad eagle's wheeling form;
> Eastward, in long perspective glittering, shine
> The wood-crowned cliffs that o'er the lake recline;
> Those lofty cliffs a hundred streams unfold,
> At once to pillars turned that flame with gold:
> Behind his sail the peasant shrinks to shun
> The west that burns like one dilated sun,
> Where in a mighty crucible expire
> The mountains, glowing hot, like coals of fire.
>
>   – *Descriptive Sketches Taken*
>   *During a Pedestrian Tour Among the Alps*

This is clearly the effort of an immensely talented twenty-year-old: look at those hundred streams unfolding, not merely glittering in the powerful, slanting rays of the sun, but *flaming*. Also, look at those mountains in the distance, glowing (and with potential for further fieriness).

But if one steps back to consider the history of poetry in English, the most achieved descriptive poetry (by, for example, Alexander Pope) had already – by now towards the end of the eighteenth century – been celebrated, and then reacted against. One gets the sense that young Wordsworth is perhaps rather strenuously reaching for the wonted wow factor. He does it well. The turbulence of the weather and the fire of the far-off mountains is stirring. There is a touch of disquietude, even alienation, about the above passage (though the poet is not yet quite reaching out of the familiar restrictions of eighteenth-century verse). As Coleridge would later put it in his *Biographia Literaria* (1817), the language is 'not only peculiar and strong, but at times knotty and contorted, as if by its own impatient strength'. As for the spectacular environment it describes, it might remind one of a scene in Peter Jackson's *Lord of the Rings* trilogy. But it is missing something, and (according to Coleridge) it is as if it knows. It is missing depth beyond description – 'mental space', to use Coleridge's phrase – in which imagination might unfold and reverberate. Wordsworth would later (having by then been under Coleridge's influence) find the words for this depth.

It was not the twenty-year-old Wordsworth of *Descriptive Sketches* who changed perceptions. It would be Wordsworth in his late twenties/early thirties – the author of the *Lyrical Ballads*, *The Prelude* and other works – who would show future writers (and their readers) – not least De Quincey (and his readers) – 'that inward eye' with which we can look more deeply into inner-space, back in time, to the formation of our minds, of ourselves, of our souls.

In his late twenties (1798-99) Wordsworth would write again about that same visit to those Alps. Gone is the crude attempt at poetic alchemy (the mountains as glowing hot coals of fire). Gone is the attempt to match the immensity of mountainous scenery with immense but familiar verbal effort. The poet is doing something different. He is remembering not so much the sights as his own keen anticipation of what might have been in store for him, say, over the next mountain-crag:

> The only track now visible was one
> That from the torrent's further brink held forth
> Conspicuous invitation to ascend
> A lofty mountain. After brief delay
> Crossing the unbridged stream, that road we took,
> And clomb with eagerness, till anxious fears
> Intruded, for we failed to overtake

Our comrades gone before.
By fortunate chance,
While every moment added doubt to doubt,
A peasant met us, from whose mouth we learned
That to the spot which had perplexed us first
We must descend, and there should find the road,
Which in the stony channel of the stream
Lay a few steps, and then along its banks;
And, that our future course, all plain to sight,
Was downwards, with the current of that stream.
Loth to believe what we so grieved to hear,
For still we had hopes that pointed to the clouds,
We questioned him again, and yet again;
But every word that from the peasant's lips
Came in reply, translated by our feelings,
Ended in this, – 'that we had crossed the Alps.'

– The Prelude VI

The thirty-year-old poet's recollection of anti-climax has replaced the youth's flaming and towering (and perhaps vainglorious) verbalising. Now in the early nineteenth century he has realised something: enormous, complex and awe-inspiring as the natural world is, it is as nothing compared to the immensity and complexity of the ever-deepening, ever-expanding *inner* life of a human being. Coleridge had already caught at the matter (though in a poem he himself would refer to as a 'fragment') as 'caverns measureless to man'. Wordsworth, however, would become the nineteenth century's chief celebrant of the soul, and *The Prelude* would have an effect as enduringly magnetic on the disappointed as it would have on the credulous.

Disappointment with the outer world – or with, for that matter, politicians' promises or one's own life – can provoke either a lashing out or a retreat inward. In young Wordsworth's mind, there had been a very painful episode of guilt and a terrible sense of being in the wrong place (back in England), despite its being the country of his birth.

> I felt the ravages of this most unnatural strife
> In my own heart; there it lay like a weight,
> At enmity with all the tenderest springs
> Of my enjoyments. I, who with the breeze
> Had played, green leaf on the blessed tree
> Of my beloved country ...
> Now from my pleasant station was cut off,
> And tossed about in whirlwinds ...
> A conflict of sensations without name,
> Of which he only who may love the sight
> Of a village steeple as I do can judge,
> When in the congregation, bending all
> To their great Father, prayers were offered up
> Or praises for our country's victories,
> And, 'mid the simple worshippers perchance
> I only, like an uninvited guest
> Whom no one owned, sate silent ...
>
> – *The Prelude* X

The feeling of displacement, and of having to contain almost intolerable personal and political contradictions, is something about Wordsworth and his work that the late Seamus Heaney has identified with strongly:

> The good place where Wordsworth's nurture happened [England, and, in particular, the Lake District] and to which his habitual feelings are most naturally attuned has become, for the revolutionary poet, the wrong place. Life, where he is situated, is not as he wants it to be. He is displaced from his own affections by a vision of the

good that is located elsewhere ... He feels like a traitor among those he knows and loves. To be true to one part of himself, he must betray another part.

(Heaney, 'Place and Displacement', 1985)

Or, to borrow Heaney's words from the end of his poem, 'The Tollund Man' (*Wintering Out*, 1972), Wordsworth 'will feel lost, unhappy and at home.'

In order to best write down these feelings of dislocation and fracture, the young, evolving Wordsworth somehow had to find the more spacious mental vantage point over the hot frictions of life lived through and felt moment by moment. But he would not find it until years later.

Wordsworth met Coleridge in 1797 and thought him the most wonderful man he had ever met. Coleridge was clearly – by all accounts (including De Quincey's, William Hazlitt's, and many others') – a 'wonderful' man. Dorothy Wordsworth recorded her first impressions:

> He is a wonderful man. His conversation teems with soul, mind and spirit ... at first I thought him very plain, that is for about three minutes; he is pale, thin, and has a wide mouth, thick lips and not very good teeth, longish, loose-growing hair, half-curling and rough. But if you hear him speak for five minutes you think no more of them.
> – Dorothy Wordsworth to an unknown correspondent, 1797

Hazlitt recollected his first impressions of Coleridge's transformative talk:

> ... it seemed to me, Sir, who was then young, as if the sounds had echoed from the bottom of the human heart, and as if that prayer might have floated in solemn silence through the universe ... I could

not have been more delighted if I had heard the music of the spheres. Poetry and Philosophy had met together, Truth and Genius had embraced, under the eye and with the sanction of Religion. This was even beyond my hopes. I returned home well satisfied ... for there was a spirit of hope and youth in all nature, that turned everything into good.

– Hazlitt, 'My First Acquaintance with Poets'[3]

Hazlitt was in the doldrums as a failed painter already at the age of seventeen, but he was electrified into activity as a writer by Coleridge. In 1797 Wordsworth was in the doldrums too. Already well-known for his public speaking, Coleridge seemed to have the secrets of life, the universe and everything (the honey dew, the milk of paradise) just at the tip of his tongue. Wordsworth was completely unknown. Coleridge seemed to have the potential to make sense of everything. He had already written 'Frost at Midnight', 'The Nightingale', *Christabel*, and the extraordinarily sumptuous, mellifluous and mystical *Kubla Khan*. Also, he was engaged in writing *The Rime of the Ancient Mariner*.

Coleridge offered Wordsworth a sense of wonder,[4] which was communicated predominantly through conversation. Coleridge was just what Wordsworth needed in 1797, as Wordsworth had become thoroughly disillusioned with the French Revolution (and the Reign of Terror). The hostilities between France and England continued to prevent him from seeing Annette and Caroline. He was perhaps, as it might be put, taken out of himself by Coleridge's immensely impressive mind. The following passage conveys

---

[3] This essay first appeared in Leigh Hunt's *Liberal* in 1823.

[4] I am indebted to Seamus Perry for his lecture, 'What did Wordsworth Make of Coleridge?' Annual Wordsworth Lecture, Institute of English Studies, University of London, 29 November 2012.

something of how inspired and inspiring Coleridge's company and conversation must have been.

> I have not only completely extricated the notions of Time, and Space; but have overthrown the doctrine of Association, as taught by Hartley, and with it all the irreligious metaphysics of modern Infidels – especially, the doctrine of Necessity. – This I have done; but I trust, that I am about to do more – namely that I shall be able to evolve all the five senses, that is, to deduce them from one sense, and to state their growth and the causes of the difference – and in this evolvement to solve the process of Life & Consciousness.
>
> – from a letter from Coleridge to Thomas Poole,
> 16 March, 1801

But Wordsworth had always much preferred being self-contained. The scared boy who once would grasp (as he would tell Isabella Fenwick in 1843) at a wall or tree to recall himself from the abyss of idealism was by now (the late 1790s) the fully-fledged side-stepper of abysses. By dint of his pondering the same thoughts his intelligence had grown sharper and his ideas had gained in maturity and precision. Hugely impressive as he found him, Wordsworth could not but hold on to a certain scepticism about Coleridge ('solve the process of Life & Consciousness' indeed).

Wordsworth may have wanted a view of life to feel at home in, and he may have wanted to feel that everything hangs together deeply and meaningfully. But while Coleridge's mind 'ached to behold and know something great – something one & indivisible' (as he put it in a letter to John Thelwall dated 14 October, 1797), for Wordsworth there was an overwhelming realisation: life was not something he could even imagine feeling at home in. Life, the universe and everything would probably never hang together deeply and meaningfully. God probably wouldn't be around to intervene – He, if present at all, seemed disturbingly blind and indifferent.

When Wordsworth and Coleridge went to Germany together in 1799, they parted company. Coleridge went to the University of Göttingen to study the German language and metaphysics. He was, he said, going to get right to the bottom of the great mystery of life through mastering the key works of the great German philosophers. His stated intention was, remember, to solve the problem of life and consciousness. Wordsworth, on the other hand, found himself isolated (with his sister Dorothy) – during the coldest winter on record – in a cottage in lonely Goslar. Holed up and with little to do other than keep warm, and with nothing much to look at, and with nobody really to talk to (other than a couple of neighbours who couldn't speak English), Wordsworth found that many memories, particularly of his childhood in the Lake District, were coming rushing back upon him with extraordinary force of colour and sound:

> – All shod with steel,
> We hiss'd along the polish'd ice, in games
> Confederate, imitative of the chace
> And woodland pleasures, the resounding horn,
> The Pack loud bellowing, and the hunted hare.
> So through the darkness and the cold we flew,
> And not a voice was idle; with the din,
> Meanwhile, the precipices rang aloud,
> The leafless trees, and every icy crag
> Tinkled like iron, while the distant hills
> Into the tumult sent an alien sound
> Of melancholy, not unnoticed, while the stars,
> Eastward, were sparkling clear, and in the west
> The orange sky of evening died away.
>
> – *The Prelude* I

The strangeness and the haunting beauty seemed to have been 'sent' from somewhere. The noise of the world in which the child Wordsworth played (as the man now realised) had been – and still was – an 'alien sound'. Even with the benefit of hindsight, nature can't necessarily be reduced to something we can understand. The alien sound has travelled through time (from the child's mind to the adult's), but instead of landing on the page in a securely connected way, and instead of delivering a meaning, it remains suspended just beyond the brink of intelligibility. *The Prelude* recognises this gap time and time again. If there is an interconnectedness of life, the universe and everything, it is not necessarily ours for the seeing, however much we ache for it.

For Coleridge, natural beauty could somehow reveal 'something great – something one & indivisible – and it is only in the faith of this that rocks or waterfalls, mountains or caverns give me the sense of sublimity or majesty!' When Wordsworth was at his lowest ebb and met Coleridge, in 1797, the sheer improbability of Coleridge's gestalt was something of a tonic. But by some point soon after they had parted company in Germany, at the turn of the century, Wordsworth found he could not remain energised by Coleridge's faith in an 'intelligible universe'.

> Oh! when I have hung
> Above the raven's nest, by knots of grass
> And half-inch fissures in the slippery rock
> But ill sustain'd, and almost, as it seem'd,
> Suspended by the blast which blew amain,
> Shouldering the naked crag; Oh! at that time,
> While on the perilous ridge I hung alone,
> With what strange utterance did the loud dry wind
> Blow through my ears! the sky seem'd not a sky
> Of earth, and with what motion mov'd the clouds!
>
> – *The Prelude* 1

Wordsworth gets verbally repetitive ('motion mov'd') because there is so little that can be done with experience that can't be understood or resolved. Another alien sound – this time a 'strange utterance' – has time-travelled from the child to the man without making itself graspable. All that the poet can do is continue to exert himself around and about the recollected experience in the fond hope that it will make sense or become comfortable or unified in some way. For Wordsworth, this (and other experiences) *won't* make sense, and *won't* become comfortable or unified. Alien presences from Wordsworth's past have unaccountably become sharpened and have begun to find their way back through to him and needle his attention in that cold cottage in Goslar. In such an urgent emerging context, the Coleridgean ache to know everything in its totality falls away like a toothache after a good dose of laudanum. The radiance of, and power in, the rush of involuntary memories overrides any ambition to dream up, or construct, or settle for, some sort of explanation of life. As Ralph Waldo Emerson would say in his 1841 essay, 'Self-Reliance', 'In every work of genius we recognize our own rejected thoughts; they come back to us with a certain alienated majesty.'

In the following passage, Wordsworth recollects abandoning his faith in a political solution to the evils of society. In his recollected twisting, turning and trying to find a way round the dilemma, he produces not a solution, but the taste by which he is to be relished – *poetry.*

So I fared,
Dragging all precepts, judgments, maxims, creeds,
Like culprits to the bar; calling the mind,
Suspiciously, to establish in plain day

Her titles and her honours; now believing,
Now disbelieving; endlessly perplexed
With impulse, motive, right and wrong, the ground
Of obligation, what the rule and whence
The sanction; till, demanding formal 'proof',
And seeking it in every thing, I lost
All feeling of conviction, and, in fine,
Sick, wearied out with contrarieties,
Yielded up moral questions in despair.

Wordsworth's sense of being lost in the labyrinth can be compared with anyone's. If Wordsworth (the Cambridge-educated, published poet) can't explain life, and can't explain what's wrong with society and how to fix it, doesn't that leave him at basically the same level as everyone else, including the uneducated Lakeland characters he has written about in the *Lyrical Ballads*? For example, the idiot boy in Wordsworth's poem of that name doesn't know what the moon is – he thinks it is the sun shining cold. The little girl in 'We Are Seven' cannot comprehend that two of her siblings have died. She thinks they merely lie in the churchyard – as if they were in bed asleep. She sings to them. And the 'Mad Mother' in the poem of that name considers herself still married to the long-absent father of her darling infant son. In many shorter lyric poems Wordsworth shows us that people without education and money can think and feel deeply. Not always correctly, but deeply. And he shows us that these individuals can discover in themselves the mental space in which they can make some sort of sense of the world – just as Wordsworth had had to make do as a young boy and was still having to make do as a man.

Here, he recollects stealing a rowing boat as a boy. He felt at the time, it would seem, inordinately guilty about this rather genteel joyride. He felt so disorientated by the guilt that he slipped into imagining he was being pursued by the shapes and shades of the natural world around him. Or perhaps the poet (having by now taken the travails of his friend's Ancient Mariner to heart) has imagined rather than remembered these feelings. Or perhaps both. At any rate he has somehow graphically re-engaged with the momentous formative processes of conscience and consciousness:

> One evening (surely I was led by her)
> I went alone into a Shepherd's Boat,
> A Skiff that to a Willow tree was tied
> Within a rocky Cave, its usual home ...
> No sooner had I sight of this small Skiff,
> Discover'd thus by unexpected chance,
> Than I unloos'd her tether and embark'd.
> The moon was up, the Lake was shining clear
> Among the hoary mountains; from the Shore
> I push'd, and struck the oars and struck again
> In cadence, and my little Boat mov'd on
> Even like a Man who walks with stately step
> Though bent on speed. It was an act of stealth
> And troubled pleasure; not without the voice
> Of mountain-echoes did my Boat move on,
> Leaving behind her still on either side
> Small circles glittering idly in the moon,
> Until they melted all into one track
> Of sparkling light...
> I dipp'd my oars into the silent Lake,
> And, as I rose upon the stroke, my Boat
> Went heaving through the water, like a Swan;
> When from behind that craggy Steep, till then
> The bound of the horizon, a huge Cliff,
> As if with voluntary power instinct,
> Uprear'd its head. I struck, and struck again

And, growing still in stature, the huge Cliff
Rose up between me and the stars, and still,
With measur'd motion, like a living thing,
Strode after me...
        ...and after I had seen
That spectacle, for many days, my brain
Work'd with a dim and undetermin'd sense
Of unknown modes of being; in my thoughts
There was a darkness, call it solitude,
Or blank desertion, no familiar shapes
Of hourly objects, images of trees,
Of sea or sky, no colours of green fields;
But huge and mighty Forms that do not live
Like living men mov'd slowly through the mind
By day and were the trouble of my dreams.

                              – *The Prelude* I

The alien presences were not going to go away again. They were, if anything, growing. And yet they were remaining as inscrutable as ever.

Having tried to collaborate with Coleridge in 1797-98, Wordsworth found that he was not prepared to share his friend's aches and aspirations. He had his own. He would instead express human experiences: 'by fitting to metrical arrangement a selection of the real language of men [and women] in a state of vivid sensation.' In the following passage (in which italics have been added) he peers back in time to the generation of a recollection. He formulates what he finds plainly yet hauntingly:

There was a Boy; ye knew him well, ye cliffs
And islands of Winander! many a time,
At evening, when the earliest stars began
To move along the edges of the hills,

Rising or setting, would he stand alone,
Beneath the trees, or by the glimmering lake;
And there, with fingers interwoven, both hands
Pressed closely palm to palm and to his mouth
Uplifted, he, as through an instrument,
Blew mimic hootings to the silent owls
That they might answer him. – And they would shout
Across the watery vale, and shout again,
Responsive to his call, with quivering peals,
And long halloos, and screams, and echoes loud
Redoubled and redoubled; concourse wild
Of jocund din! And, when there came a pause
Of silence such as baffled his best skill:
Then, sometimes, in that silence, *while he hung*
Listening, a gentle shock of mild surprise
Has carried far into his heart the voice
Of mountain-torrents; or the visible scene
Would enter unawares into his mind
With all its solemn imagery, its rocks,
Its woods, and *that uncertain heaven* received
Into the bosom of the steady lake.

                                        – *The Prelude* I

An uncertainty at odds with Christian faith seems to have been carried far into the boy's heart. (The English biologist known as 'Darwin's bulldog', Thomas Huxley, would coin the word 'agnostic' in 1869.) It seems that Wordsworth knows that in order to continue to write with such power about his boyhood, he needs to have the courage of his lack of convictions. He doesn't reach the mystical vantage point, the unity, that Coleridge ached after. And yet the ache will not go away. He can therefore empathize with other individuals, with feelings so strong yet perceptions so limited, such as the 'Mad Mother'.

Look at the first stanza. We see at first merely a woman in distress with a child. She is (with her weather-beaten appearance) clearly one of the many downtrodden and neglected individuals of no account to a philosopher or a politician:

> Her eyes are wild, her head is bare,
> The sun has burnt her coal-black hair,
> Her eye-brows have a rusty stain,
> And she came far from over the main.
> She has a baby on her arm,
> Or else she were alone ...

Yet in the next stanza, in the twinkling of an eye, we are spirited behind her eyes and entangled illuminatingly in her thoughts and feelings. She knows that people say she is mad. But she is capable of moments of clarity and, above all, love (as well as thoughts of suicide and revenge). Her mind is as bright and dendritic – and its roots as lost in the darkness – as anyone else's mind. The baby is in some sense a replacement for the lost husband.

> Dread not their taunts, my little life!
> I am thy father's wedded wife;
> And underneath the spreading tree
> We two will live in honesty.
> If his sweet boy he could forsake,
> With me he never would have stay'd:
> From him no harm my babe can take,
> But he, poor man! is wretched made,
> And every day we two will pray
> For him that's gone and far away.

It is hard not to think also that Wordsworth is painfully conscious of his own lover and daughter living on together without him, back in France, as he produces this poem, which is such an extraordinary expression of awareness of what another individual might be going through.

> "Sweet babe! they say that I am mad,
> But nay, my heart is far too glad;
> And I am happy when I sing
> Full many a sad and doleful thing ...

The reader doesn't have to have breastfed a child to appreciate Wordsworth's sense of what the special bond between mother and baby might feel like.

> Suck, little babe, oh suck again!
> It cools my blood; it cools my brain;
> Thy lips I feel them, baby! they
> Draw from my heart the pain away.
> Oh! press me with thy little hand;
> It loosens something at my chest;
> About that tight and deadly band
> I feel thy little fingers press'd.
> The breeze I see is in the tree;
> It comes to cool my babe and me.
> Oh! love me, love me, little boy!
> Thou art thy mother's only joy ...

As Wordsworth knows all too well, the repetition ('Suck ... suck'; 'cools ... cools'; 'love me, love me') is what any human being – not least himself – will produce on the surface when stirred to the depths. Like this poor woman, Wordsworth has lived, thought and felt amidst beautiful natural scenery. His mind, like hers (and ours), interacts with nature, but s/he does not understand it in a comprehensive way. S/he only understand it in her/his own way –

the only understanding a human being can have.

> I'll teach my boy the sweetest things;
> I'll teach him how the owlet sings.
> My little babe! thy lips are still,
> And thou hast almost suck'd thy fill.
> – Where art thou gone my own dear child?

When Wordsworth folded his own agonies and ecstasies (remembered and imagined) into poetry, he created the taste by which he would be relished. There would be no reader anywhere on earth who would relish the taste of Wordsworth's poetry more than Thomas De Quincey.

3 ◆ Wordsworth's Number One Fan: Thomas Penson Quincey, budding addict, outlaw, scholar, writer

Thomas Penson Quincey – later Thomas De Quincey – was born in Manchester on 15 August 1785. He was the fourth of eight children. His father was 'a merchant ... in the English sense ... that is, he was a man engaged in *foreign* commerce and no other.' (Morrison, 89) Hence, De Quincey's sense of himself – as mixing a little with alien natures despite himself – was passed on to him from his father. De Quincey said that the 'expansive love' that characterised him and his favourite sister, Elizabeth, came to them from their father.

> These remarks are particularly illuminating, for they explain both
> the faint atmosphere of unreality that hangs round the mild,
> receding features of Thomas Quincey [senior] and also his son's

evident feeling that, in spite of this ghostliness, his father was a man eminently worthy of a love which his unenthusiastic temperament perhaps had not the power of eliciting to the full.

– Sackville-West, 3

Oddly for a trader in the West Indies, Thomas Quincey was a 'conscientious protester' against slavery. He died at the age of forty from tuberculosis. (Frances Wilson, *Guilty Thing*, 23) De Quincey would spend his entire adult life expecting to die of tuberculosis too; and then, having himself lived for decades longer than his father, he would attribute his own longevity to laudanum, to which he was addicted (as the medical profession has since called it) all his adult life. It was to De Quincey as if the 'fierce chemistry' of his opium dreams continually reconstituted and rekindled the life-force in him, and practically doubled the number of years he might otherwise have got in this world.

His mother, 'although an attentive mother, inspired more irritation than love in her children.' (Sackville-West, 4) She has almost invariably, with a touch of misogynistic contempt, been characterised as a 'lady architect' (a familiar female target related perhaps to the much-abused blue stocking); and Greenhay, as the family house was called, was her big project. Her children 'grew up around stonemasons, carpenters, painters, plasterers and bell-hangers; while other women of her class busied themselves with gentler pursuits, Elizabeth Quincey demolished walls and improved views, expanded floors and widened windows.' (Wilson, *Guilty Thing*, 14) This may or may not have had something to do with the fact that two of her four sons ran away from home, one to Wales, the other to sea.

A miniature painted after her marriage has suggested, to some commentators, something disagreeable about her. For example, De Quincey's biographer, Edward Sackville-West, has said 'It is not a very pleasing face: a certain hard fixity in the eyes, a general lack of sensitiveness in the bold, handsome features, delineate a nature uncompromising and obtuse.' (Sackville-West, 5) Here, it is possible that Sackville-West has written in mediumistic obedience to that most eloquent spokesman for victims of strict mothers everywhere, Lord Byron: 'Some women use their tongues – She looked a lecture.' (*Don Juan*, I, xv) At any rate, readers of De Quincey, and Sackville-West's biography of him, are to understand that Mrs Quincey's contribution to the world's production of children who feel bad about themselves has been exemplary. 'Trial by jury, English laws of evidence, all were forgotten; and we were found guilty on the bare affidavit of the angry accuser.' De Quincey grew up believing – or said he grew up believing – himself to be a criminal.

It is compelling to speculate that Oscar Wilde's belief, that there is 'no essential incongruity between crime and culture' (Wilson, *Guilty Thing*, 341), can be traced all the way back to De Quincey's vivid sense of responsibility for the catalogue of ills that had befallen his family. As a child, he felt to blame for any praise his intelligence might receive. 'Usually mothers defend their own cubs right or wrong,' he remembered. 'Not so my mother.' Should a visitor or a tutor compliment one of her children, Mrs Quincey would not show any pride, but she would protest 'so solemnly ... that we children held it a point of filial duty to believe ourselves the very scum and refuse of the universe.' (Alexander Japp, *Memorials*, I, 9-10) In fairness to De Quincey's mother, it may have been under the pressure of a widow's anxieties that she spoke and acted unjustly. Thus, by a peculiar cruelty of fate, had she but known it, she was really losing her children – who 'missed something and dwelt upon the want of it, and on the utter coldness and precision of her endearments' (Japp, *Memorials*, I, 11) – as well as her husband. The De Quincey siblings were coming to rely more and more exclusively on each other for all that made life bearable; to have confidence only in each other. They were already learning to lie to her.

One's lies can somehow look a little whiter in the context of one's already-established criminality. Whatever had made the house a home had failed Mrs Quincey's children; everything except one another. De Quincey and his favourite sister, Elizabeth, drew together – as would happen with De Quincey and other girls in the future – as two frightened strays huddling together for warmth in a bleak world.

4 ♦ Thomas De Quincey unfolding

the greatest event in the unfolding of my mind
— De Quincey remembers his discovery of Wordsworth and
Coleridge's *Lyrical Ballads* at the age of fifteen in 1799

The word 'unfolding' has a double meaning. A bud unfolds into a blossom, but the boat which one teaches children to make by folding paper unfolds into a flat sheet of paper. The second kind of 'unfolding' is really appropriate to parable; the reader takes pleasure in smoothing it out so that he has the meaning on the palm of his hand.
— Walter Benjamin, 1934

At some point or other in adolescence, the individual might emerge from the depths of his formative years. He might just reach out, get a hold of whatever external advantages he can, set about transitioning into adulthood, and live a fulfilling life. For example, he might complete his education, take holy orders, become an educationalist, and get married and raise a family, like Derwent Coleridge. Or alternatively he might scorn his inherited privileges and live instead by his own light. For example, rather than becoming a landowning Tory peer like his father, he might instead insist publicly on the necessity of atheism, get himself expelled from Oxford University, run away to continental Europe with a couple of schoolgirls, and spend the rest of his life as a radical poet and polemicist, like Shelley.

In 'about the year 1799', two years before deciding to run away himself, the fifteen-year-old Thomas De Quincey experienced 'the greatest event in the unfolding of my own mind' (Morrison, *English Opium Eater*, 34), and from there began the inner journey of the most eloquent autobiographer, biographer, critic and congenital hanger-on in English literature. The poetry that seemed now to offer him the way out of the restrictions of home, homework and his mother's evangelicalism was by living poets: Wordsworth and Coleridge. On reading, rereading, and effectively being shown the way to a better quality of consciousness by Wordsworth and Coleridge's *Lyrical Ballads*, De Quincey was a bit like Dante following Virgil (with the difference that, in the myth, though Virgil remained always very protective of Dante, it would, in reality, turn out that Wordsworth and Coleridge did not care about De Quincey).

Having by the age of fifteen been buffeted by bewilderment,

desire and despair, De Quincey already bore the marks of ostracism and eccentricity. 'For I was the shiest of children, and a natural sense of personal dignity held me back at all stages of life, from exposing the least ray of feelings which I was not encouraged *wholly* to reveal.' (Morrison, 95) Wordsworth and Coleridge's poetry seemed to conduct De Quincey back to the depths of himself, including his subconscious memories. He would never fail to recognise this region as his lifelong resource as a writer, including his work as a critic. As Fred Burwick has put it, 'In his criticism of Wordsworth's poetry, he identified the subconscious as that arena out of which the conscious mind draws its power.' (Burwick, 160) Here, in the subterranean convolutions of soul and poetry was all he would ever need to write about.

> ... a growth
> Of intertwisted fibres serpentine
> Up-coiling, and inveterately convolved
> — Wordsworth, 'Yew-Trees', 1815

5 ◆ De Quincey Rooted in England

> For very shame you must away!
> "What? not yet seen the coast of France!
> The folks will swear, for lack of bail,
> You've spent your last five years in jail!'
> Keep moving! Steam, or Gas, or Stage,
> Hold, cabin, steerage, hencoop's cage —
> Tour, Journey, Voyage, Lounge, Ride, Walk,
> Skim, Sketch, Excursion, Travel-talk —
> For move you must! 'Tis now the rage,

The law and fashion of the Age.
                    – Coleridge,'The Delinquent Travellers', 1824

Apart from a visit to Ireland in the summer of 1800, De Quincey would never travel abroad like Wordsworth, Coleridge, Byron, Keats or Shelley. His 'aversion to travel' (Japp, *Memorials*, II, 236) was well known to his family and friends. As Alexander Japp, acquainted with De Quincey's daughter personally, said:

> Mrs [Florence] Baird Smith [De Quincey's daughter] informs me that it was one of the childlike foibles of her father to allow himself to be interestedly enlisted in the talk of his guests about visits to foreign places, and that he would often advance to the point of speaking as though it were possible for him to join his friends in their excursions on the Continent – many of the historical places and scenes in which he much wished to see. He had actually at one time made up his mind to go with Mr. Wight – who was himself a literary man – to Paris, just as he had made up his mind to accompany Mr. J.T. Field to many places; but he never actually set out on any of these excursions.
>   – Japp, *Memorials*, II, 236

Traveller's tips – such as travel light and don't believe everything you're told, drink the water, but sparingly at first until you build up immunity to its foreign properties, observe local customs and respect local gods, see as well as sightsee, avoid the black market, don't be superior or aloof, but don't try to dress like the natives either, and remember that becoming one of them is impossible – may have worked for Mary Wollstonecraft in Scandinavia, or Mungo Park in Africa up to a point, but they were beside the point when it came to De Quincey's travels in his own interior.

In one of his early self-portraits, dated 5 May 1803, he is already refining into view for himself a brooding, perceiving and presiding consciousness (for whom mere *travel* would seem virtually irrelevant):

> Last night too I image myself looking through a glass. 'What do you see?' I see a man in the dim and shadowy perspective and (as it were) in a dream. He passes along in silence, and the hues of sorrow appear on his countenance. Who is he? 'A man darkly wonderful – above the beings of this world; but whether that shadow of him, which you saw, be ye shadow of a man long since passed away or of one yet hid in futurity, I may not tell you. There is something gloomily great in him; he wraps himself up in the dark recesses of his own soul; he looks over all mankind of all tongues – languages – and nations "with an angel's ken"; but his fate is misery such as ye world knoweth not; and upon his latter days (and truly on his whole life) sit deep clouds of mystery and darkness and silence'.
>
> – Eaton, *A Diary of Thomas De Quincey, 1803*, 156

This is clearly the posturing of an avid young reader of Gothic fiction; and it is also the boy's imitation of Coleridge, who had found, by the time of the 1800 *Lyrical Ballads*, what the literary biographer Richard Holmes has called 'the authority of his poetic failure' (in contrast to Wordsworth's 'authority of poetic success'). Holmes, therefore, has inadvertently illuminated De Quincey as much as Coleridge:

> Digging back into his own mind and beliefs, he found the beginnings of a new literary identity, the poet-philosopher in a mist, whose very bafflement and intellectual frustrations gave him a new form of Romantic subject-matter ... Failure, prostration, imaginative crisis, itself became something upon which he, as a writer, could exercise brilliant lines of poetic enquiry and self-dramatisation. At times, he could even see himself as his own Mariner – 'Mid shipwrecked by storms of doubt, now mastless, rudderless, shattered, – pulling in the dead swell of a dark & windless Sea'
>
> – Holmes, *Coleridge: Early Visions*, 300-01

6 ♦ Rooted in Pain

> ... the terrific grief which I passed through drove a shaft for me
> into the worlds of death and darkness which never again closed,
> and through which it might be said that I ascended and descended
> at will, according to the temper of my spirits. Some of the
> phenomena developed in my dream-scenery, undoubtedly, do but
> repeat the experiences of childhood; and others seem likely to have
> been growths and fructifications from seeds at that time sown.
>
> – De Quincey, *Suspiria de Profundis*

In a letter dated 8 July 1854, just five years before his death, De
Quincey would be apologising (typically) to one of his many
neglected correspondents that 'I suffer now, and have long suffered,
from such a shattering of the nervous system as causes a sense of
distraction, and even of horror, to connect itself with the manual
act of writing – or indeed with any act requiring a close effort of
attention.' (Japp, *Memorials*, II, 237) De Quincey, the scholar-
journalist failing to make his way happily in the world, had been
providing utterly gripping accounts of what was going on in his
own inner world – hic sunt dracones – for decades, as the following
passage shows:

> I have been every night ... transported into Asiatic scenes. I know
> not whether others share in my feelings on this point; but I have
> often thought that if I were compelled to forego England, and to
> live in China, and among Chinese manners and modes of life and
> scenery, I should go mad. The causes of my horror lie deep; and
> some of them must be common to others. Southern Asia, in general,
> is the seat of awful images and associations. As the cradle of the
> human race, it would alone have a dim and reverential feeling
> connected with it. But there are other reasons. No man can pretend
> that the wild, barbarous, and capricious superstitions of Africa, or

of savage tribes elsewhere, affect him in the way that he is affected
by the ancient, monumental, cruel, and elaborate religions of
Indostan, &c. The mere antiquity of Asiatic things, of their
institutions, histories, modes of faith, &c. is so impressive, that to
me the vast age of the race and name overpowers the sense of youth
in the individual. A young Chinese seems to me an antediluvian
man renewed. Even Englishmen, though not bred in any knowledge
of such institutions, cannot but shudder at the mystic sublimity of
castes that have flowed apart, and refused to mix, through such
immemorial tracts of time; nor can any man fail to be awed by the
names of the Ganges, or the Euphrates. It contributes much to
these feelings, that southern Asia is, and has been for thousands of
years, the part of the earth most swarming with human life; the
great *officina gentium* [workshop of peoples]. Man is a weed in
those regions ... I am terrified by the modes of life, by the manners,
and the barrier of utter abhorrence, and want of sympathy, placed
between us by feelings deeper than I can analyze. I could sooner
live with lunatics, or brute animals.

    – De Quincey, *Confessions of an English Opium-Eater*

The eternal, cancerous and *un*utterable ordeal has thus been
uttered. De Quincey has catered for English magazine-readers by
conflating the two most reputedly infernal regions – Hell and the
East. The language is so ravishing, precise, unpredictable, and
viscerally xenophobic that it feels almost immersive:

All this, and much more than I can say, or have time to say, the
reader must enter into before he can comprehend the unimaginable
horror which these dreams of oriental imagery, and mythological
tortures, impressed upon me. Under the connecting feeling of
tropical heat and vertical sun-lights I brought together all creatures,
birds, beasts, reptiles, all trees and plants, usages and appearances,
that are found in all tropical regions, and assembled them together
in China or Indostan. From kindred feelings, I soon brought Egypt

and all her gods under the same law. I was stared at, hooted at,
grinned at, chattered at, by monkeys, by paroquets, by cockatoos. I
ran into pagodas, and was fixed for centuries at the summit or in
secret rooms: I was the idol; I was the priest; I was worshipped; I
was sacrificed. I fled from the wrath of Brama through all the forests
of Asia: Vishnu hated me: Seeva laid wait for me. I came suddenly
upon Isis and Osiris: I had done a deed, they said, which the ibis
and the crocodile trembled at. I was buried for a thousand years in
stone coffins, with mummies and sphynxes, in narrow chambers
at the heart of eternal pyramids. I was kissed, with cancerous kisses,
by crocodiles; and laid, confounded with all unutterable slimy
things, amongst reeds and Nilotic mud.

– De Quincey, *Confessions of an English Opium-Eater*

The English psychonaut demonstrates, directly and flamboyantly,
how he shuffled off the coil of the wimpy kid and invested himself
with the power of scholarly distinction. 'At thirteen I wrote Greek
with ease; and at fifteen my command of that language was so
great, that I not only composed Greek verses in lyric metres, but
could converse in Greek fluently, and without embarrassment –
an accomplishment which I have not since met with in any scholar
of my times' (Morrison, 8). He is more than merely a sick man or
a madman. He is an Olympian scholar *and* sufferer; and, like a
shaman, he can cure others as well. By the age of fifteen his special
intellectual supremacy was established, as he says early on in his
Confessions: 'That boy,' said Rev Nathaniel Morgan (Headmaster
of Bath Grammar School) about De Quincey in the late 1790s
(Morrison, 266), 'could harangue an Athenian mob, better than
you or I could address an English one.' (Morrison, 8)

De Quincey is a sick man who has healed himself. He is cured.
He has been transmuted by an initiation – Oriental in its ferocity
– into the mysteries of the mind and the cosmos. He must

shamanise in order to remain cured. Writing in the past tense, he shows readers how he has endured, survived and self-improved – by reaching right down and risking inner experience:

> The cursed crocodile became to me the object of more horror than almost all the rest. I was compelled to live with him; and (as was always the case almost in my dreams) for centuries. I escaped sometimes, and found myself in Chinese houses, with cane tables, &c. All the feet of the tables, sophas, &c. soon became instinct with life: the abominable head of the crocodile, and his leering eyes, looked out at me, multiplied into a thousand repetitions: and I stood loathing and fascinated.
> – De Quincey, *Confessions of an English Opium-Eater*

Even as he makes it back to waking consciousness of his beloved children, he can find no comfort or security in their presence even in broad daylight, with the crawling chaos right at his back:

> And so often did this hideous reptile haunt my dreams, that many times the very same dream was broken up in the very same way: I heard gentle voices speaking to me (I hear every thing when I am sleeping); and instantly I awoke: it was broad noon; and my children were standing, hand in hand, at my bed-side, come to show me their coloured shoes, or new frocks, or to let me see them dressed for going out. I protest that so awful was the transition from the damned crocodile, and the other unutterable monsters and abortions of my dreams, to the sight of innocent *human* natures and of infancy, that, in the mighty and sudden revulsion of mind, I wept, and could not forbear it, as I kissed their faces.
> – De Quincey, *Confessions of an English Opium-Eater*

His description and interpretation of 'the path along which he has travelled to his present authoritative station' (James Vigus, 'Teach yourself guides to the literary life, 1817-1825: Coleridge, De

Quincey, and Lamb', 153) was catnip for a class of reader on the rise – the armchair spiritual tourist.

7 ♦ Some Furious Romancing a la Coleridge

> But the truth is, that inaccuracy as to facts and citations from books was in Coleridge a mere necessity of nature ... Not three days ago ... I found my old feelings upon the subject refreshed by an instance that is irresistibly comic, since everything that Coleridge had relied upon as a citation from a book in support of his own hypothesis, turns out to be a pure fabrication of his own dreams; though, doubtless (which indeed it is that constitutes the characteristic interest of the case), without a suspicion on his part of his own furious romancing.
>
> – De Quincey, *Confessions of an English Opium-Eater*

For all the brio of his performance of himself in every sentence, De Quincey wasn't often greatly exercised by a need for factual accuracy. For example, as Robert Morrison has pointed out, the passage about De Quincey's children at his bedside cannot be literally true:

> De Quincey dates this dream 'May 1818', but it clearly haunted him for months. 'Children', in any event, could not have stood at his bedside in May 1818 because at that time the De Quinceys had only one child, William. Their second child, Margaret, was not born until 5 June 1818, and of course it would have been some time before she was able to stand beside her brother.
>
> – Morrison, 291

Behind the De Quincey façade life seems rather illusory, an

alchemical and improbable sequence of events. In his opium dreams it seemed to him sometimes that in exquisite raiment and to the delicate sound of flutes, the sins of the world were passing in dumb show before him, 'drawn out, by the fierce chemistry of my dreams, into insufferable splendour that fretted my heart.' (Morrison, 67)

For readers of *Confessions* in the nineteenth century, things they had dreamed of were suddenly made real by language that was more *per*formative than *in*formative. Things of which they had never even dreamed were revealed to them with De Quincey's 'extemporaneous excitement' (Wright, 24). Like the other great English Romantics, he used language not so much to inform as to actualise. Confined to communicating via the flat of the page (or, to borrow from Wordsworth, the barren leaf),[5] his achievement was in bringing into blossom such a soulful new vision. He achieved it so airily and yet so convincingly. Thus Baudelaire, in his 'Preliminary Confession' section of *Artificial Paradises* (1860), would assure the reader, 'in all good faith, that the rising curtain will reveal nothing short of the most astonishing, most complex, and most splendid vision that the writer's fragile instrument has ever illuminated upon the snow-white page.' (Diamond, 101)

As Morrison has put it, 'in interweaving drugs and the city, despair, and genius, De Quincey initiated the literature of addiction, and its portrait of the modern artist on a quest that begins with insidious promises of transcendence, but is soon vitiated by consumerism, disembodiment, and deadening repetition' (Morrison, *English Opium Eater*, 397-8). So, De Quincey did not

---

[5] 'Enough of Science and of Art; / Close up those barren leaves', as Wordsworth proclaims in 'The Tables Turned'.

just disappear into inner space. More outrageous in tone than Coleridge, but less daring in intellectual substance, he made of the laudanum bottle a sort of microscope through which he showed readers their own souls under industrial capitalism.

8 ◆ Romantic Agony Privatised and Publicised

'Thus when the universal sun has set does the moth seek the lamplight of privacy.'
— Karl Marx, doctoral thesis, Berlin University

De Quincey wanted the seclusion of a scholar in a cottage. He did not want to write for a living (or so he said). He didn't have to until the age of thirty-six:

In 1821 ... I went up to London avowedly for the purpose of exercising my pen, as the one source then open to me for extricating myself from a special embarrassment (failing which case of dire necessity, I believe that I should never have written a line for the press).
— Morrison, 262

He had to work in the hurly-burly of journalism that was orienting much of itself in accordance with the appetites of a public that was not classically educated:

In order to excuse the tone (which occasionally I may be obliged to assume) of one speaking as from a station of knowledge to others having no knowledge, I beg it to be understood that I take that station deliberately, on no conceit of superiority to my readers, but as a companion adapting my services to the wants of those who need them.
— Goldman, 171

He had to write popular articles because he had used up all the money his father had left him and it had become unavoidable for him – bibliophile, drinker, drug user, husband and father as he was – to correspond with and get commissioned by magazine editors in order to keep the wolf (if not the crocodile) from the door. He found that he could publish his articles and get paid for them; indeed, he found sometimes that he could get paid for his articles before writing them. (Then, as now, the dynamics of editorial carrot and stick could vary.)

During the first half of the nineteenth century, magazines and newspapers were proliferating at an unprecedented rate in Great Britain. Their readerships consisted increasingly of people with little or no classical education, and this presented opportunities for their contributors to appear more scholarly than they actually were – like crafty mountebanks impressing impressionable Dalesmen in the village square; or even a bit like that 'gentleman of somewhat dashing exterior', though known by his visiting card as 'The Hon. Augustus Hope' (supposedly 'a brother of Lord Hopetoun's'), yet with 'a tang of vulgarity' (Wright, 67) discernible only by the one or two locals with enough exposure to upper class culture to know.

This gentleman, though recognised by Coleridge as 'grossly ungrammatical in his ordinary conversation' (Wright, 67), had the temerity to frank his letters by that false name, and thence 'nobody presumed to question his pretentions any longer; and, henceforward, he went to all places with the consideration attached to an Earl's brother. All doors flew open at his approach' (Wright 67). It was perhaps with something of this bounder's resolve and resourcefulness that a new kind of journalist could hornswoggle

and entertain readers. De Quincey, most famously the author of
*Confessions of an English Opium-Eater: Being an Extract From
the Life of a Scholar*, has been alleged by some of his more classically
confident critics to be in some ways the unreal thing, deceptive if
not deceitful, but certainly untrustworthy and not quite what he
appears to be; a light skirmisher rather than a true scholar.

9 ◆ Romantic Agony Conserved

When it first appeared in 1821, *Confessions* caused a sensation,
and it has retained and renewed its cultural (and medical)
significance ever since. It has never been out of print. By the middle
of the nineteenth century Baudelaire was practically making it a
textbook for the dandy,[6] the decadent, the *flâneur* – the dreamy,
amoral and alienated observer of the modern urban scene. The
memoir recounts the exotic – yet (as De Quincey took pains to
put across) peculiarly English – practices and pleasures of a restless
scholar in search of an elusive ideal.

Having abandoned in his teens any ambition he had had of
becoming a poet, he was now, as a prose stylist – and arguably also
a crude copyist of Wordsworth and Coleridge – situated somewhere

---

[6]'Which of us, in his moments of ambition, has not dreamed of a poetic
prose, musical, without rhythm and without rhyme, supple enough and
rugged enough to adapt itself to the lyrical impulses of the soul, the
undulations of reverie, the jibes of conscience? It was, above all, out of my
exploration of huge cities, out of the medley of their innumerable
interrelations, that this haunting ideal was born.'
– Baudelaire, Dedication to *Small Prose Poems*, 1862

between playfulness and poetry. His biographer, Grevel Lindop, a poet himself, has written about him with a poet's understanding: 'He was very prone to obsessive, repetitive thought carried to the point of mental fatigue. His life had been lived in a continual climate of anxiety palliated by ambition and private fantasy.' (Lindop, *Opium-Eater*, 223)

There is a sense that with De Quincey Wordsworth's and Coleridge's ideas have degenerated. Edward Sackville-West has suggested that this degeneration has been the result of 'four evil qualities' which 'preponderate dismayingly' in De Quincey's writing: 'Pedantry, Digression, Prolixity, and Facetiousness.' For Sackville-West:

> These bad fairies were present at De Quincey's birth, and they may be said to have been largely successful in encompassing his ruin; for, if the bulk of his work is so little read today, the responsibility must be laid at their door.
>
> – Sackville-West, 240-1

In his neurotic sensibility and his passion for novelty, De Quincey foreshadows every unhappy, solitary hero of the twentieth century, such as Camus's Stranger or H.P. Lovecraft's Outsider; he has something of the anguish of modern times. In his opening paragraph to *Suspiria de Profundis*, he evokes the general uproar of the great industrialised world, and then he draws the reader right inside the haunted space behind the eyes of any thinking inhabitant of that world:

> Already, in this year 1845, what by the procession through fifty years of mighty revolutions amongst the kingdoms of the earth, what by the continual development of vast physical agencies – steam in all its applications, light getting under harness as a slave for man,

powers from heaven descending upon education and accelerations of the press, powers from hell (as it might seem, but these also celestial) coming round upon artillery and the forces of destruction – the eye of the calmest observer is troubled; the brain is haunted as if by some jealousy of ghostly beings moving amongst us; as it becomes too evident that, unless this colossal pace of advance can be retarded, (a thing not to be expected,) or, which is happily more probable, can be met by counter-forces of corresponding magnitude, forces in the direction of religion or profound philosophy, that shall radiate centrifugally against the storm of life so perilously centripetal towards the vortex of the merely human, left to itself the natural tendency of so chaotic a tumult must be to evil; for some minds to lunacy, for others to a reagency of fleshly torpor. How much this fierce condition of eternal hurry, upon an arena too exclusively human in its interests, is likely to defeat the grandeur which is latent in all men, may be seen in the ordinary effect from living too constantly in varied company. The word *dissipation*, in one of its uses, expresses that effect; the action of thought and feeling is too much dissipated and squandered. To reconstitute them into meditative habits, a necessity is felt by all observing persons for sometimes retiring from crowds. No man ever will unfold the capacities of his own intellect who does not at least chequer his life with solitude.

– Morrison, 81-2

However, having spent many years as a writer utilising the scraps of solitude available to him in a world where one is too often 'Distracted from distraction by distraction' (as *another* good Coleridgean, T.S. Eliot, would put it in *Four Quartets*), De Quincey seems almost as agitated in his inwardness as anyone else might be in the uproarious material world. Writing to fellow magazine contributor Mary Russell Mitford in 1846, when he was sixty-one, he was still expressing a self-contained misery with a hint of Milton's Satan:

No purpose could be answered by my vainly endeavouring to make intelligible for my daughters what I cannot make intelligible for myself – the indecipherable horror that night and day broods over my nervous system. One effect of this is to cause, at certain intervals, such whirlwinds of impatience as precipitate me violently, whether I will or not, into acts that would seem insanities, but are not such in fact, as my understanding is never under any delusion. Whatever I may be writing becomes suddenly overspread with a dark frenzy of horror. I am using words, perhaps, that are tautologic; but it is because no language can give expression to the sudden storm of frightful revelations opening upon me from an eternity not coming, but past and irrevocable. Whatever I may have been writing is suddenly wrapt, as it were, in one sheet of consuming fire – the very paper is poisoned to my eyes. I cannot endure to look at it, and I sweep it away into vast piles of unfinished letters, or inchoate [sic] essays begun and interrupted under circumstances the same in kind, though differing unaccountably in degree. I live quite alone in my study, so nobody witnesses these paroxysms. Nor, if they did, would my outward appearance testify to the dreadful transport within.

– Japp, *Thomas De Quincey: His Life and Writings*, I, 340

In poems, letters and notebooks, Coleridge had already written in comparably plangent and shivery terms on the same subject before De Quincey. Way after De Quincey's time, and even after Mario Praz, in *The Romantic Agony* (1933), had taken cognisance of the great cry that had come from the depths through the Romantics, the steadily un-histrionic George Orwell would air (albeit in cooler, lighter language) some of the fears and frustrations of the struggling writer.[7]

Whatever stripe your politics or whatever shade your metaphysics, if you use booze/fags/drugs and write for a living, negotiating the edifice of life and work by middle-age tends to feel, from the inside out, like living your very own season in hell. In this respect, De Quincey is the Romantic writer *par excellence*. Taking him at his own self-justifying estimation (predicated on a renunciation of the pains that drove him to opium rather than the opium itself), he becomes the very archetype of the romanticisation of excess resisted by historiographers.

10 ◆ Romantic Agonies Believed or Balanced

His self-expression is so often so resplendent that the need for a balanced view can somehow make the path of negation seem like the only way to go. In short, his more exacting critics have found him rather hard to believe. To take it that the sentences that he wrote really do transmit the truth about the life of Thomas De Quincey (and the lives of those other individuals he wrote about) would be to behave, for example, as if Derrida's angel of Deconstruction had never passed over the world of letters. De Quincey – like Coleridge, as he always reminds us when it suits

---

[7](see previous page)'In a cold but stuffy bed-sitting room littered with cigarette ends and half-empty cups of tea, a man in a moth-eaten dressing-gown sits at a rickety table, trying to find room for his typewriter among the piles of dusty papers that surround it. He cannot throw the papers away because the wastepaper basket is already overflowing, and besides, somewhere among the unanswered letters and unpaid bills it is possible that there is a cheque for two guineas which he is nearly certain he forgot to pay into the bank. There are also letters with addresses which ought to be entered in his address book. He has lost his address book, and the thought of looking for it, or indeed of looking for anything, afflicts him with acute suicidal impulses.' (Orwell, 'Confessions of a Book Reviewer', 1946)

him to – is always more likely to allege himself to have seen a ghost than actually prove a point of fact:

> Coleridge was of opinion that, if a man were really and *consciously* to see an apparition – supposing, I mean, the case to be a physical possibility that a spiritual essence should be liable to the action of material organs – in such circumstances death would be the inevitable result.
>
> – Wright, 127

There have been quite a few books and articles written, if not to explode, then at least to stay cautious and academically credible about, De Quincey's De Quincey; to interrogate at least, if not manage to lay bare entirely, the conceit. Some of these critiques, though tart, have been useful. Albert Goldman warned readers against taking De Quincey's scholarly 'pretensions at their face value' and inferring 'from his legitimate achievements powers and capacities that he did not actually possess' (Goldman, *The Mine and the Mint*, 162-3). On the one hand, this is sensible advice. Professional critics know of course that there is no point in being naive, which is why they so often remember that it is safer to rid oneself of the whole tangle of flowers and weeds than it is to risk being caught gullibly admiring the flowers. On the other hand, Frances Wilson – whose distaste for De Quincey as a man is clear, yet whose relish of the dendritic mind runs deep – has recently encouraged readers (familiar, doubtless, with Twitter, Instagram, Facebook and the science of self-exposure) all the way back in again by saying 'We are all De Quinceyan now' (Wilson, *Guilty Thing*, 342)

11 ♦ We Are All De Quinceyan

And he – like us – was like Coleridge, and like Hamlet: he could have been bounded in a nutshell and counted himself a king of infinite space, were it not that he had bad dreams. He (Hamlet, Coleridge, We) will never be free from the depths. His prisoner's-eye view of 'the deep deep tragedies of infancy' seems to have become an important part of what Psychology as a new academic discipline would teach people in the twentieth century about what goes on in the depths of human nature: ' ... and when the child's hands were unlinked for ever from his mother's neck, or his lips for ever from his sister's kisses, these remain lurking below all, and these lurk to the last. Alchemy there is none of passion or disease that can scorch away these immortal impresses.' (Morrison, 137)

He would never recover from the shock of his sister Elizabeth's death when he was a child, and he would linger weirdly over the details of her dead body for decades. He had been bullied for years by his elder brother, and his only means of defence was to become the abject of such snivelling victimhood that no bully on earth would want to continue tormenting him:

> I had a perfect craze for being despised. I doted on it; and considered contempt a sort of luxury that I was in continual fear of losing. Why not? Wherefore should any rational person shrink from contempt, if it happen to form the tenure by which he holds his repose in life? ... to me, at that era of life, it formed the main guarantee of an unmolested repose ... The slightest approach to any favourable construction of my intellectual pretensions alarmed me beyond measure; because it pledged me in a manner with the hearer to support this first attempt by a second, by a third, by a

fourth – O Heavens! there is no saying how far the horrid man might go in his unreasonable demands on me ... Professing the most absolute bankruptcy from the very beginning ... I never could be made miserable by unknown responsibilities.

Sally Shuttleworth has handled this unhappily formative episode in De Quincey's life sympathetically:

> The 'world of strife' his brother creates is as far removed as possible from the image, created in later-century fiction for children, of siblings harmoniously entering an enchanted land. De Quincey's brother was 'as full of quarrel as it is possible to imagine', and dragged De Quincey into daily fights, both within the material world, and against factory boys, and in the imaginative world of their personal creation:
>
> > I lived for ever under the terror of two separate wars in two separate worlds: one against the factory boys, in a real world of flesh and blood, of stones and brickbats, of flight and pursuit, that were anything but figurative: the other in a world purely aerial, where all the combats and the sufferings were absolute moonshine.
>
> His sufferings from the former, however, were as nothing compared to those from 'that dream kingdom which rose like vapour from my own brain'. Their jointly imagined kingdom merely intensifies his persecution, providing a more threatening arena in which his brother can exercise his will to power.
>
> – Sally Shuttleworth, *The Mind of the Child*, 80

So, his sister Elizabeth's death haunted him, his eldest brother had been inside his head for years causing irreparable damage, and his mother taught him he was worthless.

Yet the poetry he discovered at the age of fifteen gave profound meaning to those very depths of psychological trauma. And, on top of that, it helped De Quincey anatomise the neurosis that had shaken and sharpened him into his peculiar perceptiveness. That poetry, so beautiful and meaningful, though not to be learned from through a series of logical steps, brought "'the ray of a new morning", and an absolute revelation of untrodden worlds, teeming with power and beauty, as yet unsuspected amongst men' (Morrison, *English Opium Eater*, 35). With that hunger of the mind – and with feelings of expansion and curiosity familiar to anyone who has ever contemplated C.S. Lewis's Wardrobe, or J.K. Rowling's Platform $9^{3/4}$ – he wanted to tread those worlds himself.

12 ◆ We Are Seven

There was, for example, Wordsworth's poem 'We Are Seven' about a poor and uneducated little cottage girl whose brother, John, and sister, Jane, are dead and buried. She sings to them at their graveside every day. As she does so, she knits her stockings and hems her kerchief. The speaker of the poem, apparently a well-heeled gentleman with university-honed scepticism, cannot understand her. Why is she talking and behaving as if the dead are present? Why does she sit and sing to them? It seems a sorry and even slightly embarrassing business for this man – who, after all, has doubtless undergone an expensive process of learning that has resulted in enhanced mental capability – to have his perambulations interrupted in order to explain to an eight-year-old that the dead don't exist. Her parents really ought to have corrected her by now. They really ought to have explained to their little girl the basic fact of the separation of life and death. And if they had at least tried, and she still didn't understand, she ought perhaps to have been beaten or sent to bed without any supper until she cottoned on. Of course, her parents (and their parents before them) probably didn't know any better either. It would have taken a heart of stone not to sympathise in quiet with the life of this little girl.

Finding himself confounded by the great recalcitrance handed down through the generations of the poor (when he might better have felt himself chafed at last by direct contact with the great mystery), the speaker has found his familiar power of speech denied. He has been reduced to repetition and 'throwing words away': 'But they are dead; those two are dead!' By this point in the poem the reader knows that the little girl is not now, and nor was she ever, inferior to the speaker. She is an entirely new type of individual to appear in eighteenth century literature. (*Lyrical Ballads* first appeared in 1798.) She is not some amusing rapscallion (to be found in a play by Goldsmith or a novel by Fielding) running rings around the old reactionary with the airs and graces. But she does prevail, and she does have the final say, with a broadly unsettling self-assurance. The loneliness and the raw company of the rural environment, with the hills around and the clouds above, has not falsified experience for her in the way that wooden chairs, tables and teachers do in the classroom. She has been entirely untouched by the conversations, lectures, sermons, pamphlets and books of churchmen, politicians, professors, or any other contemporary worthies. There is an uncultivated brightness and beauty about her that makes her seem like an emanation of the time and place:

Her hair was thick with many a curl
That clustered round her head.

She had a rustic, woodland air,
And she was wildly clad:
Her eyes were fair, and very fair;
– Her beauty made me glad.

– Wordsworth, 'We Are Seven'

Her colour, movement, freshness and vitality somehow find their way through to, and even dwell in the imagination of, the speaker. The repetition ('fair, and very fair') suggests something about the girl just beyond the man's comprehension yet needling his attention like a fishbone. The dash ('–') is like the opening of the speaker's heart and mind; and then there is the straight recognition of the real power of the girl's 'beauty', and the effect it has on the beholder. The effect is a bit perplexing. Perhaps it has something in it of the desire to possess her in some way. Any feeling of being possessed by her is unthinkable to such a man. But maybe something of the feeling is there. The hard edges of his literalness seem to have been softened as from the inside out, and more is conveyed by the girl's narrative than the bare information of numbers. For the growing, unschooled girl, her siblings' reality is inseparable from her love for them. And why does she love them? Who knows the answer to a question no child ever asks, love being so spontaneous and so simple when one is a child? It is not that these siblings have tastes in common, though they have had a world in common. Perhaps such relationships are a blessed gift of nature while human beings are still within their nature. No ambitious Oxbridge student preparing for his final exams could afford to stoop anywhere near such a lived reality let alone feel it. The type of mind that can appreciate such a poem is not the mind hemmed in by conventional education, but it is much more likely to be the type of mind that is willing to have its sense of mystery deepened by contact with reality and its sense of reality deepened by contact with mystery.

13 ◆ Seven in All

Young De Quincey was willing to have his senses of mystery and reality recognised as inextricable and deepened. He understood this little girl. He knew exactly what it is like to lose a sister in childhood. The knowledge of the experience was folded up in him. The first sister he lost in childhood was called Jane. The poem must therefore have seemed to De Quincey to recognise him and reach for him out of the fabulous dark:

> 'The first that died was sister Jane;
> In bed she moaning lay,
> Till God released her of her pain;
> And then she went away.
>
> 'So in the church-yard she was laid;
> And, when the grass was dry,
> Together round her grave we played,
> My brother John and I.
>
> 'And when the ground was white with snow,
> And I could run and slide,
> My brother John was forced to go,
> And he lies by her side.'
>
> — Wordsworth, 'We Are Seven'

Decades later, in *Suspiria de Profundis*, De Quincey would recollect his own sister Jane's death:

> So passed away from earth one out of those sisters that made up my nursery playmates; and so did my acquaintance (if such it could be called) commence with mortality. Yet, in fact, I knew little more of mortality than that Jane had disappeared. She had gone away; but, perhaps, she would come back. Happy interval of heaven-born ignorance! Gracious immunity of infancy from sorrow disproportioned to its strength! I was sad for Jane's absence. But still in my heart I trusted that she would come again. Summer and winter came again – crocuses and roses; why not little Jane?
>
> – Morrison, 92-3

After the loss of Jane, 'the first wound in my infant heart' was healed easily enough (Morrison, 93). But the next loss, of Elizabeth, was the big one, and it would be with a Wordsworthian sense of the mysterious osmosis of love and understanding between children that De Quincey would cling to and conserve her memory. In *Suspiria* he asks: 'But what was it that drew my heart, by gravitation so strong, to my sister?' (Morrison, 94). He answers his own question, first by saying that it was not the fineness of Elizabeth's mind. 'Serene and capacious as her mind appeared to me upon after review, was *that* a charm for stealing away the heart of an infant? Oh, no!' (Morrison, 94). It must have been something much stronger than intellectual ability that made him treasure Elizabeth, 'my leader and companion' (Morrison, 95), so dearly. 'Hadst thou been an idiot, my sister, not the less I must have loved thee – having that capacious heart overflowing, even as mine overflowed, with tenderness, and stung, even as mine was stung, by the necessity of being loved ... That lamp lighted in Paradise was kindled for me which shone so steadily in thee; and never but to thee only, never again since thy departure, *durst* I utter the feelings which possessed me.' (Morrison, 94-5) When De Quincey read Wordsworth's *Lyrical Ballads* for the first time, he felt that he was reading his own life. He would never lose the feeling, especially when it came to his writing his own life.

14 ◆ At Sixes and Sevens

His terrestrial concerns, however, thickened inevitably as he aged. In the 1840s and 1850s his creditors chased him as much in waking life as the crocodiles chased him in his dreams. He had always been a bit like Coleridge's anguished Mariner:

> Like one, that on a lonely road
>   Doth walk in fear and dread,
> And having once turn'd round, walks on
>   And turns no more his head:
> Because he knows, a frightful fiend
>   Doth close behind him tread.
> — *The Rime of the Ancient Mariner*

But, of course, by now all De Quincey's sufferings had the framework of profound meaning provided originally by the poetry of Wordsworth and Coleridge. His daughter Florence said of him:

> It was an accepted fact among us that he was able when saturated with opium to persuade himself and delighted to persuade himself (the excitement of terror was a real delight to him) that he was dogged by dark and mysterious foes, at the same time the persuasion gave a sanction to his conscience for getting away from the crowded

> discomfort of a home without any competent head ... where ... he
> could by no possibility have done any work had he remained.
> – Spice, 'The Animalcule', *London Review of Books*, 5

Ever since his diary entry of June 1803, he had long been in the habit of fusing his own personal feelings with those of Coleridge to create an amalgam, the two halves of which he remained keen to combine to form an indistinguishable whole:

> I walk home thinking of *Coleridge* – am in transports of love and
> admiration for him ... go to bed ... still thinking of Coleridge who
> strikes me (as I believe he always did) with a resemblance to my
> mysterious character (a compound of Ancient Marinere and Bath
> concert room traveller with bushy hair); – I begin to think him the
> greatest man that has ever lived and go to sleep ...

He, like Coleridge, considered himself a philosopher, and, like Coleridge, promised paradigm-shifting works of philosophy that never appeared, for example, *De Emendatione Humani Intellectus* ('On the Correction of the Human Intellect') after Spinoza's unfinished *Tractatus de Intellectus Emendatione*. The magnitude of this task was conducive to procrastination: 'under the banner of "philosophy", he was free to pursue the miscellaneous reading which had always been his delight.' (Lindop, *Opium-Eater*, 189) Albert Goldman has said that this pursuit suited De Quincey because he was 'both idle and proud' (Goldman, 18). But wasn't De Quincey's life (before having to take up his pen at the age of thirty-six) the 'convenient state of mind' (Goldman, 18) of the man of wealth and taste? Wasn't it the condition aspired to, or envied by, the ever-increasing population of magazine readers and novel readers of the nineteenth century? De Quincey was like Walter Scott's young

Edward Waverley,[8] the English gentleman of honour who by his sixteenth year had the advanced habits of abstraction and love of solitude that could only – as we (all De Quinceyan now) might fondly suppose – be found in an individual avowedly *not* concerned with factories, *not* involved in grasping industrial activities, and *not* 'allied to ... detestable commerce' (Morrison, *English Opium Eater*, 60).

15 ♦ What manner man art thou?

Forthwith this frame of mine was wrench'd
   With a woeful agony,
Which forc'd me to begin my tale
   And then it left me free.

Since then at an uncertain hour,
   Now oftimes and now fewer,

---

[8]'With a desire of amusement ... Waverley drove through the sea of books like a vessel without a pilot or a rudder. Nothing perhaps increases by indulgence more than a desultory habit of reading, especially under such opportunities of gratifying it. I believe one reason why such numerous instances of erudition occur among the lower ranks is, that, with the same powers of mind, the poor student is limited to a narrow circle for indulging his passion for books, and must necessarily make himself master of the few he possesses ere he can acquire more. Edward, on the contrary, like the epicure who only deigned to take a single morsel from the sunny side of a peach, read no volume a moment after it ceased to excite his curiosity or interest; and it necessarily happened, that the habit of seeking only this sort of gratification rendered it daily more difficult of attainment, till the passion for reading, like other strong appetites, produced by indulgence a sort of satiety.' (*Waverley*, Chapter 3, 15)

> That anguish comes and makes me tell
> My ghastly aventure.
>
> I pass, like night, from land to land;
> I have strange power of speech;
> The moment that his face I see
> I know the man that must hear me;
> To him my tale I teach.
>   – *The Rime of the Ancient Mariner*

Some critics – including his own mother – cross-examined De Quincey as to the identity and morality of *Confessions* but he said nothing necessarily believable about its morality or immorality. It looks, though, for all the world like he told the truth about his drug experiences. For example, having eulogized opium in a way that might otherwise come across as a bit on the sniggering and parodic side, he says:

> But if I talk in this way, the reader will think I am laughing: and I can assure him, that nobody will laugh long who deals much with opium: its pleasures even are of a grave and solemn complexion; and in his happiest state the opium-eater cannot present himself in the character of *l'Allegro*: even then, he speaks and thinks as becomes *Il Penseroso*.
>   – Morrison, 39

The British public, left to draw its own conclusions, still probably decided that the author of the notorious *Confessions* must be, if not a hedonist or a depraved individual, then certainly 'a mandarin Romantic, an enervate drop out improvising sonorous prose canticles from dreams and hallucinations induced by the laudanum-bottle' (Wright, 9).

In an 1824 edition of the *Family Oracle of Health*, an anonymous commentator said that the 'use of opium has been much increased by a wild, absurd, and romancing production, called the *Confessions of an English Opium-Eater.* We observe, that at some late inquests this wicked book has been severely censured, as the source of misery and torment, and even of suicide itself, to those who have been seduced to take opium by its lying stories about celestial dreams, and similar nonsense.' (Morrison, *English Opium Eater*, 211) Only a few people knew that in fact he was a struggling writer of modest means, and a disappointed, and indeed embittered, disciple of Wordsworth and Coleridge, and still living and writing in their shadows.

He would continue to be regarded as a Romantic figure, despite having written and published so much of his work, including the masterly *Suspiria*, during the Victorian era. His style, for one thing, was too colourful, too individual for a good Victorian Realist. And the impact of that account of his first opium hit with the reading public – 'oh! Heavens! what a revulsion! what an upheaving, from its lowest depths, of the inner spirit! what an apocalypse of the world within me!' (Morrison, 39) – was not easily forgotten:

> That my pains had vanished was now a trifle in my eyes: - this negative effect was swallowed up in the immensity of those positive effects which had opened before me – in the abyss of divine enjoyment thus suddenly revealed. Here was a panacea ... for all human woes: here was the secret of happiness, about which philosophers had disputed for so many years, at once discovered: happiness might now be bought for a penny, and carried in the waistcoat pocket: portable ecstasies might be corked up in a pint bottle: and peace of mind could be sent down in gallons by the mail coach.
>
> – Morrison, 39

In the most compelling passages of his writing, all pretence of objectivity was abandoned, and the speaker seemed to stand revealed as De Quincey in the thinnest of disguises. Borges would call it De Quincey's 'self-novelisation' (Spice, 8). Whatever it is, it has a lot more De Quincey in it than those readers unprepared to accept his *Confessions as* confessions have conceded. When Charles Lamb teased De Quincey in his good-humoured way about the *Confessions*, and in particular the Oxford Street passages, De Quincey reacted in a way surely evident of touched nerves:

> 'There are', said he, 'certain places & events & circumstances, which have been mixed up or connected with parts of my life which have been very unfortunate, and these, from constant meditation & reflection upon them, have obtained with me a sort of sacredness, & become associated with solemn feelings so that I cannot bear without the greatest mental agony to advert to the subject, or to hear it adverted to by others in any tone of levity or witticism.'
>
> – Morrison, *English Opium Eater*, 212

What is more, the speaker would often admit to odd fancies that seemed even odder in their context. For example, he offered his playfully solipsistic 'doctrine of the true church on the subject of opium: of which church I acknowledge myself to be the only member – the alpha and the omega' (Morrison, 42). The alpha and the omega are the first and last letters of the Greek alphabet, and this proudly exceptional Grecian, who performs himself in every sentence he writes, is discoursing on his own performance of himself in every sentence he writes. It may be, or seem, the kind of mirror-trickery that seems merely to entertain – if not outright irritate – readers, and that is precisely why it is valuable: the writer has succeeded somehow in sending the full blossom of his personality through the flat black and white page. What we lack in factual clarity he has made up for in his pursuit of a *jeu d'esprit*, to see where it leads, and perhaps to question whatever beliefs about ourselves we hold fast to. We all metabolise sensation. We all consume and pollute. We all remember and misremember. We all try to manage the world's reception of our warts and all when we cannot erase them. To echo again De Quincey's latest biographer, Frances Wilson, 'we are all De Quinceyan now'.

16 ◆ Budding Philosopher, Flourishing Flɐneur

If English Romanticism had not advanced up a blind alley and run its head into a wall (by the 1810s Wordsworth was a tax collector and Coleridge had begun to put it about that he had never really been all that radical),[9] De Quincey himself decided on an ambitious attempt to shake off preconceived ideas, to extend the scope of the literary essay, to introduce into it art, science, history: in a word, to use this form of literature as a frame in which to insert more serious work. The fantasy was, as he told his mother in 1818,

> ... that, by long and painful labour combining with such faculties as God had given me, I might become the intellectual benefactor of my species. I hoped and have every year hoped with better grounds that, (if I should be blessed with life sufficient) I should accomplish a great revolution in the intellectual condition of the world; that I

[9]For example, Alan Vardy calls the *Biographia Literaria* 'Coleridge's most obvious act of reinvention' (*Constructing Coleridge: The Posthumous Life of the Author*, 2010, 5).

should both as one cause and as one effect of that revolution place education upon a new footing, throughout all civilized nations, was but one part of this revolution: it was also but a part (though it may seem singly more than enough for a whole) to be the first founder of true Philosophy.

– Japp, *Memorials*, II, 111

The actual result looked much more like journalistic improvisation and, until late in his life, merely a lot of essays scattered up and down the back numbers of various periodicals. In this respect, again, when he wrote of Coleridge, it must have been himself he had in mind too:

Assuredly, Coleridge deserved, beyond all other men that were ever connected with the daily press, to be regarded with distinction. Worlds of fine feeling lie buried in that vast abyss, never to be disentombed or restored to human admiration. Like the sea it has swallowed treasures without end, that no diving bell will bring up again. But nowhere throughout its shoreless magazines of wealth, does there lie such a bed of pearls confounded with the rubbish and 'purgamenta' of ages, as in the political papers of Coleridge ...
– *Works of Thomas De Quincey*, edited by Grevel Lindop, volume 10, 319

Confessions was originally conceived as an esoteric extension of Wordsworth's long autobiographical poem, *The Prelude* (which was not published until 1850, but read by De Quincey in manuscript form in the 1810s). De Quincey's speaker would be, however, more cultured, more damaged, more glamorous and more refined than Wordsworth's plainer and mentally healthier speaker. De Quincey's speaker discovered in artificiality a specific for the feeling of alienation inspired by the worries of life and the coarsening manners of his time; and, in the 1840s, when De

Quincey was continuing to transform and *opiate* his childhood reminiscences in *Suspiria*, Wordsworth was writing sonnets on the punishment of death and complaining about the unhappy result of northern England's ever-improving railway system: the thickening presence of the great unwashed in the Lake District – those pestilential tourists and weekenders from places such as Leeds and Manchester.

With the Industrial Revolution taking its full, clamorous and increasingly connecting strides, one imagines the Opium-Eater winging his way to the land of dreams, seeking refuge in extravagant illusions, living alone and apart, far from the world of his contemporaries, in an atmosphere suggestive of more cordial epochs and less odious surroundings:

> Paint me, then, a room ... Make it populous with books: and, furthermore, paint me a good fire; and furniture, plain and modest, befitting the unpretending cottage of a scholar. And, near the fire, paint me a tea-table; and ... place ... two cups and saucers on the tea tray ... paint me an eternal tea-pot ... paint me a lovely young woman, sitting at the table. Paint her arms like Hebe's.— But no ... not even in jest let me insinuate that my power to illuminate my cottage rests upon a tenure so perishable as mere personal beauty, or that the witchcraft of angelic smiles lies within the empire of any earthly pencil.
>
> – Morrison, 60

That is, helped to by De Quincey himself, one can *imagine* him in 'plain', 'modest' and 'unpretending' circumstances, even though one *knows* differently. Where Wordsworth had sought satisfaction in the simple, or natural, things of life (such as the unconventional wisdom in little girls, idiot boys and old leech-gatherers), the outlaw figure of *Confessions* would resort to the artificial and the exotic;

where Wordsworth had needed to put some distance between himself and Coleridgean metaphysics once he had learned all he needed in that department, De Quincey continued to recognise in Coleridge a kindred spirit *au fait* with opium, otherworldly pursuits, and unnatural – and even perverse – pleasures and pains.

17 ◆ From the Buds of May to the Flowers of Evil

> Whither is fled the visionary gleam?
> Where is it now, the glory and the dream?
> — Wordsworth, 'Intimations of Immortality'

If De Quincey and Wordsworth went opposite ways in their pursuit of meaning (the former towards, the latter away from, the sphere of Coleridge's influence), the result of their quest was to be the same in each case, broadly speaking: disillusionment.

De Quincey was not just a refined reincarnation of Wordsworth; *The Rime of the Ancient Mariner* played a huge part in confirming the central importance to him of guilt and trauma, *Kubla Khan* helped confirm the magic of opium-assisted writing, and the *Biographia Literaria* confirmed that Germany had produced the philosophers from whom it was most worth an English metaphysician's while borrowing, and stealing. 'I will assert finally that ... [I have] read for thirty years in the same track as Coleridge – that track in which few of any age will ever follow us, such as German metaphysicians, Latin schoolmen, thaumaturgic Platonists, religious Mystics.' (Wright, 40-1) When De Quincey published his essays on Coleridge, it did not look obviously as if it was in the most admiring, sympathetic and sincere good faith that he retailed to his readership what he had seen and heard in Coleridge's company:

> Nobody who knew him ever thought of depending on any appointment he might make: spite of his uniformly honourable intentions, nobody attached any weight to his *in re futura*: those who asked him to dinner or any other party, as a matter of course, sent a carriage for him, and went personally or by proxy to fetch him; and, as to letters, unless the address were in some female hand that commanded his esteem, he tossed them all into one *dead letter bureau*, and rarely, I believe, opened them at all.
>
> – Wright, 14

Whether it was retailed in good faith or bad, De Quincey made good use of the older poet's information, and all the bizarre aspects of his behaviour – the unhappy marriage, the opium habit and the plagiarisms appeared, suitably adapted and embellished, in 'Coleridge' (*Tait's Edinburgh Magazine*, 1834). Coleridge's daughter, Sara Coleridge, was understandably annoyed when the public was effectively being encouraged to identify her recently deceased father with De Quincey's unhealthy version of 'Coleridge' in De Quincey's own image. But she did see that:

> Of all the censors of Mr Coleridge, Mr De Quincey is the one whose remarks are the most worthy of attention; those of the rest in general are but views taken from a distance, and filled up by conjecture, views taken though a medium, so thick with *opinion*, even if not clouded with vanity and self love, that it resembles a horn more than glass or the transparent air. The Opium-Eater, as he has called himself, had sufficient inward sympathy with the subject of his criticism to be capable in some degree of beholding his mind, as it actually existed, in all the intermingling shades of individual reality;

and in few minds have these shades been more subtly intermingled than in my father.

– Wright, 15

Sara's balanced view has been massively, though quietly, influential. De Quincey, like Coleridge, 'lived the life of the mind, which fed on distinctions, and Wordsworth the life of the spirit, which was nourished by certainties ... His blacks and whites bothered De Quincey, and De Quincey's shifting grays annoyed him.' (Wright, 12).

Coleridge's influence on *Confessions* is everywhere apparent, from the very title and theme of the book, inspired by the addict's endless enslavement to the cycle of drug-taking and guilt about it:

> the powerless will
> Still baffled, and yet burning still!
> Desire with loathing strangely mixed
> On wild or hateful objects fixed.
> Fantastic passions! maddening brawl!
> And shame and terror over all!
> Deeds to be hid which were not hid,
> Which all confused I could not know
> Whether I suffered, or I did:
> For all seemed guilt, remorse or woe,
> My own or others still the same
> Life-stifling fear, soul-stifling shame.
>
> – Coleridge, 'The Pains of Sleep'

Details, such as the nightmare of being 'stared at, hooted at, grinned at, chattered at' and being 'buried, for a thousand years, in stone coffins ... in narrow chambers at the heart of eternal pyramids', and being 'kissed, with cancerous kisses, by crocodiles; and confounded with all unutterable slimy things' (Morrison, 73), have obviously been suggested by Coleridge's 'slimy things' that 'did crawl with legs/Upon the slimy sea' (*The Rime*), 'viper thoughts, that coil around my mind' ('Dejection: an Ode') and 'the fiendish crowd/Of shapes and thoughts that tortured me' ('The Pains of Sleep'). Moreover, the spirit of Coleridge's *Biographia Literaria* pervades De Quincey's *Suspiria*, the concept of the interrelatedness of poetical and philosophical texts being pushed to its furthest limits in the vivid episode of the 'higher faculty of an electric aptitude for seizing analogies', which is reminiscent of De Quincey's prose on Charles Lloyd's 'fine aerial speculations, subtle as gossamer ... lead[ing] him off into abstractions even too remote from flesh and blood' (Wright, 319):

> Rarely do things perish from my memory that are worth remembering. Rubbish dies instantly. Hence it happens that passages in Latin and English poets, which I never could have read but once (and *that* thirty years ago), often begin to blossom anew when I am lying awake, unable to sleep. I become a distinguished compositor in the darkness and, with my aerial composing-stick, sometimes I 'set up' half a page of verses, that would be tolerably correct if collated with that volume which I never had in my hand but once. I mention this in no spirit of boasting. Far from it: for, on the contrary, among my mortifications have been compliments to my memory, when, in fact, any compliment that I had merited was due to the higher faculty of an electric aptitude for seizing analogies, and by means of those aerial pontoons passing like lightning from one topic to another.
>
> – Morrison, 109

De Quincey's raptor-like propensity for looting the wilder cliff-top eyries of intellectual speculation and mixing their eggs with his own embryonic ideas is what makes *Confessions* and *Suspiria*

such nourishing omelettes. When De Quincey writes of 'the
simultaneity of arrangement under the past events of life – though
in fact successive – [that] had formed the dread line of revelation'
(Morrison, 137), he is with this single image anticipating Freud
and Jung in that he shows us our deepest energies (and our lack of
control over them):

> A pall, deep as oblivion, had been thrown by life over every trace of
> these experiences; and yet suddenly, at a silent command, at the
> signal of a blazing rocket sent up from the brain, the pall draws up,
> and the whole depths of the theatre are exposed.
>   – Morrison, 137

18 ◆ Beware! Beware!

De Quincey's autobiographical writing is sculptural, in the round,
and gestural in a way that keeps the Coleridgean sphere of influence
dense and connected, even as it dilates. It cannot be read as an
affirmation of the normal, but rather as providing the acceleration
and inspirational dynamism to transport the reader to a magical
somewhere else, beyond the single definitive version in grey print
(often so inimical to imagination), beyond the literalisation (by
printing and publishing machinery) of the life of the mind, beyond
contemporary scholars of Oxford and sellers of oxen,[10] to
somewhere like the timeless 'mental space' in which Coleridge

---

[10]'If a man "whose talk is of oxen," should become an Opium-eater, the
probability is, that (if he is not too dull to dream at all) – he will dream about
oxen' (Morrison, 6).

could enjoy himself with Edmund Spenser:

> Observe.. the exceeding vividness of Spenser's descriptions. They
> are not, in the true sense of the word, picturesque; but are composed
> of a wondrous series of images, as in our dreams ... in the domains
> neither of history or geography ... ignorant of all artificial boundary,
> all material obstacles ... truly in a land of Faery, that is, of mental
> space. The poet has placed you in a dream, a charmed sleep, and
> you neither wish, nor have the power, to inquire where you are, or
> how you got there. It reminds me of some lines of my own ...
> – *The Literary Remains of Samuel Taylor Coleridge*, collected
> and edited by Henry Nelson Coleridge, volume 1, 1836, 93-4

Just as Coleridge had stood out against the age as the individual
with the wisdom and wizardry to, for example, access Spenser's
twilit world as a poetic home from home, so De Quincey styles
himself as the scholar, shape-shifter and shoplifter who can see
himself in Coleridge and Coleridge in himself. The following
passage illustrates the double-exposure:

> Coleridge [De Quincey] spun daily and at all hours, for mere
> amusement of his [De Quincey's] own activities, and from the loom
> of his magical brain, theories more gorgeous by far, and supported
> by a pomp and luxury of images, such as Schelling – no nor any
> German that ever breathed, [though perhaps just one other English
> opium-eater] ... – could have emulated in his dreams. With the
> riches of El Dorado lying about him, he would condescend to filch
> a handful of gold from any man whose purse he fancied.
> – Wright, 40

It was from Coleridge that De Quincey derived many of his aesthetic
beliefs and literary opinions; it was Coleridge too who, in his anxiety
to focus disciples' attention away from his own weak and suffering
self towards Wordsworth and his superior craftsmanship as a poet,

had inspired De Quincey to do the same.

As for Charles Lamb, who might appear at first to have had no influence on *Confessions*, it should be remembered that in his 'Confessions of a Drunkard' (1813) the humour of the writer and the tragedy of the addict combined most compellingly for a readership increasingly acclimatising to confessional literature. De Quincey expressed a warm admiration for Lamb, and readers of *Confessions of an English Opium-Eater* may also recall the disarming manner in which Lamb's 'Drunkard' could wear his heart on his sleeve ('Why should I hesitate to declare, that the man of whom I speak is myself? I have no puling apology to make to mankind. I see them all one way or another deviating from the pure reason'), and how he foreshadows the opium-eater's direct and entertaining appeal to the reader, as if somehow aside from the narrative:

> You will think, perhaps, that I am too confidential and communicative of my own private history. It may be so. But my way of writing is rather to think aloud, and follow my own humours, than much consider who is listening to me; and, if I stop to consider what is proper to be said to this or that person, I shall soon come to doubt whether any part at all is proper.
>
> – Morrison, 62

To the end of his life De Quincey was to remain more faithful to the Romantic ideal (and of careful and conscientious documentation of his dream life and darker self) than he was to the task of replicating in words his daylight realities. The subject and scope of *Confessions* and *Suspiria* in particular called for research and detailed self-analysis. Some of the 'field-work' to which every Realist was accustomed was involved, and it took De

Quincey back to Oxford Street and Soho, as well as the inns and coffee-houses of Covent Garden where he took to writing his *Confessions*. (During the writing he left the manuscript stained with the rims of wine glasses.) Then, the nature of De Quincey's opium habit (not known then, as now, as 'addiction') necessitated a study of the relevant medical textbooks. And finally, to cover the vast range of De Quincey's interests, one would have to consult many specialist treatises on diverse subjects, in order to begin to see how he picked out unusual details or startling opinions and recast them in the mould of his own distinctive style. How successfully he used this technique can be judged from the fact that his articles on other writers and philosophers (such as Pope and Kant) earned him the reputation of a brilliant if sometimes perverse scholar, and only in 1965 did Albert Goldman reveal that some of them had been cunningly adapted (for example, in the case of the piece on Kant, from E.A. Wasianski).

When one reads *Confessions* there may be the suspicion in the reader that the whole thing is just a literary leg-pull. Edgar Allan Poe said that the *Confessions* were 'composed by my pet baboon, Juniper, over a rummer of Hollands[?] and water' (Morrison, *English Opium Eater*, 211). Or worse, disorganised, vain, and morally lax: 'The work is written throughout in the tone of apology for a secret, selfish, suicidal debauchery', declared the *Eclectic Review*: 'it is the physical suffering consequent upon it, that alone excites in the writer a moment's regret' (Morrison, *English Opium Eater*, 210).

19 ♦ *Confessions*: A Miracle of Rare Device

The indignation of the critics was more than matched by the enthusiasm of the admirers. Thus, James Mackintosh 'read the second part ... with more delight than I know how to express.' Nearly twenty-five years later, George Gilfillan noted that the *Confessions* 'took the public by storm. Its popularity was immediate and boundless, nor, even yet, has it declined.' The *Imperial Magazine* described the *Confessions* as produced by a 'mind gifted with first-rate talents.' The *Album* 'thought it one of the most interesting, and certainly the very most extraordinary, production that we had ever seen' (Morrison, *English Opium Eater*, 210). Shelley's publisher, Charles Ollier, complimented Taylor 'upon having "the best prose writer in England" for a contributor' (Morrison, *English Opium Eater*, 211).

Many authors owed a great deal to De Quincey, as any student of modern literature in English can testify. H.P. Lovecraft's vision of the city of New York, in 'He' (a short story written during 10 and 11 August 1925, as Lovecraft went on a solitary all-night walk), has more than a dash of De Quincey's shuddering disgust at people from the East:

> Garish daylight shewed only squalor and alienage and the noxious elephantiasis of climbing, spreading stone where the moon had hinted of loveliness and elder magic; and the throngs of people that seethed through the flume-like streets were squat, swarthy strangers with hardened faces and narrow eyes, shrewd strangers without dreams and without kinship to the scenes about them, who could never mean aught to a blue-eyed man of the old folk, with the love of fair green lanes and white New England village steeples in his heart ... there came a shuddering blankness and ineffable loneliness;

and I saw at last a fearful truth which no one had ever dared to
breathe before – the unwhisperable secret of secrets – the fact that
this city of stone and stridor is not a sentient perpetuation of Old
New York ... but ... it is in fact quite dead, its sprawling body
imperfectly embalmed and infested with queer animate things which
have nothing to do with it as it was in life. Upon making this
discovery I ceased to sleep comfortably ...

– Lovecraft, 141

Will Self's speaker's 'Escher-vision',[11] allowing him 'constantly
to perceive the dimensional conundrum that perception presents'
('Lizard', *Grey Area*, 47), is not unlike De Quincey's Piranesi-vision.
The economy of Self's speaker's inner life echoes De Quincey's:

When I was younger I could not focus on anything, or even
apprehend a single thought, without feeling driven to incorporate
it into some architectonic, some Great Design. I was also plagued
by lusts, both fleshly and demonic, which sent me into such dizzying
spirals of self-negation that I was compelled to narcotics.

– 'Lizard', *Grey Area*, 46

Arguably, the 'architectonic', the 'Great Design' to which De
Quincey felt driven to devoting his thoughts was an essentially
racist one, that had presumably been dropped into the aspiring
mind of the nineteenth-century magazine-reader by a God white,
Protestant and English:

His [De Quincey's] display of omniscience, the pontifical tone, the
constant self-congratulations, the mysterious hints of enormous
hidden knowledge on faraway subjects ... are not only
temperamental failings, but must be explained by conformity to
the tone of the magazines for which De Quincey wrote, and the

---

[11]Escher's 1953 lithograph, 'Relativity', is an excellent example.

hopes which he had to raise in editors and readers.
– René Wellek, *Confrontations: Studies in the Intellectual and Literary Relations Between Germany, England and the United States During the Nineteenth Century*, Chapter 4: 'De Quincey's Status in the History of Ideas', 151

That said, French literature, too, has the English Opium-Eater's pattern in its carpet. In Baudelaire's short story, 'La Fanfarlo' (1847), the protagonist Samuel Cramer is, like De Quincey, 'a sickly and fantastic creature ... the god of impotence – a modern and hermaphrodite god – an impotence so colossal and enormous that it has become epic!' There are many instances of De Quincey's influence as obvious as this, but the total number of his literary progeny is incalculable: almost every unhappy, solitary hero of a twentieth-century novel could probably trace his or her descent back to the writer with the love of opium that until 1821 did not speak its name.

20 ◆ The Little Actor

As if his whole vocation
Were endless imitation.
– Wordsworth, 'Intimations of Immortality'

There were critics who maintained that De Quincey was just a sort of caricature of Coleridge. Crabb Robinson, on reading the first part of the *Confessions*, said that the work 'must be by De Quincey. It is a fragment of autobiography in emulation of Coleridge's diseased egotism.' (Morrison, *English Opium Eater,*

211) The flaw in this theory lies in the fact that De Quincey was such a master of self-portraiture. If he lacked Coleridge's ingenuousness, he shared his neurotic sensibility and his passion for metaphysics.

De Quincey's work indeed forms an integral and important part of the great spiritual autobiography represented in the English Romantics' works – they show the efforts made by one character to achieve happiness in various forms of spiritual and physical escapism. Thus, in *Confessions* the 'poor friendless child, apparently ten years old', who 'seemed hunger-bitten', and who clung to young De Quincey in the moneylender's rat-infested lodgings, seems to be one of the characters who might well not have really existed – one of those Wordsworthian little girls that De Quincey has had enter and exit the glass of his life-writing darkly. It is as if he has cooked up some combination or other of his memory and/or desire and injected it into space, leaving readers with no literal truth they can recognise from another source, and nothing more tangible than the residue of the narrative:

> This house I have already described as a large one; it stands in a conspicuous situation, and in a well-known part of London. Many of my readers will have passed it, I doubt not, within a few hours of reading this. For myself, I never fail to visit it when business draws me to London; about ten o'clock, this very night, August 15, 1821, being my birthday – I turned aside from my evening walk, down Oxford-street, purposely to take a glance at it: it is now occupied by a respectable family; and, by the lights in the front drawing-room, I observed a domestic party, assembled perhaps at tea, and apparently cheerful and gay. Marvellous contrast in my eyes to the darkness – cold – silence – and desolation of that same house eighteen years ago, when its nightly occupants were one famishing scholar, and a neglected child – Her, by the bye, in after years, I

vainly endeavoured to trace ... I loved the child because she was my partner in wretchedness. If she is now living, she is probably a mother, with children of her own; but, as I have said, I could never trace her.

— Morrison, 20-1

Like Prospero, aware of the true ambiguity and equilibrium of being alive and in the world, De Quincey knows that:

> These our actors,
> As I foretold you, were all spirits and
> Are melted into air, into thin air:
> And, like the baseless fabric of this vision,
> The cloud-capp'd towers, the gorgeous palaces,
> The solemn temples, the great globe itself,
> Ye all which it inherit, shall dissolve
> And, like this insubstantial pageant faded,
> Leave not a rack behind. We are such stuff
> As dreams are made on, and our little life
> Is rounded with a sleep.

— *The Tempest*, IV, i

If his early, scholarly hopes had been disappointed, by the time he came to write *Suspiria* he had long learned his lesson: the section of *Suspiria* entitled 'The Palimpsest' asserts that escapism is futile and wrong – one should accept suffering willingly in expiation of one's own sins: 'Everlasting layers of ideas, images, feelings, have fallen upon your brain as softly as light. Each succession has seemed to bury all that went before. And yet in reality not one has been extinguished.' (Morrison, 135)

21 ◆ A Prognosis of Spiritual Affliction

> Thou, whose exterior semblance doth belie
>   Thy soul's immensity;
> Thou best philosopher, who yet dost keep
> Thy heritage, thou eye among the blind,
> That, deaf and silent, read'st the eternal deep,
> Haunted for ever by the eternal mind, –
>   Mighty prophet! Seer blest!
>   On whom those truths do rest,
> Which we are toiling all our lives to find,
> In darkness lost, the darkness of the grave ...
>   – Wordsworth, 'Intimations of Immortality'

De Quincey is the harbinger of the so-called Decadence, that movement in France and England characterised by a delight in the perverse and artificial, a craving for new and complex sensations, a desire to extend the boundaries of emotional and spiritual experience. He had hoped that he was writing for a readership big enough to help him out of financial trouble; he would, however, have thousands of enthusiastic readers who made *Confessions* their Bible and bedside book – not only because it mirrored their Romantic ideas and aspirations, but also because it revealed and consecrated a new and exciting literature, the literature of Wordsworth and Coleridge (in the first half of the nineteenth century), and Baudelaire, Beardsley and Wilde (in the second).

One of De Quincey's achievements is to have imagined, or predicted, an alternative literary canon. Just as in *Confessions* he championed Shelley in defiance of public and critical opinion, so in other pieces, with the same unerring skill, he singled out the then neglected authors whom we regard as the most important English writers of his time. Arthur Symons's memorable *aperçu* about J.K Huysmans's *À Rebours* – 'the breviary of the Decadence' – could be tweaked ever so slightly to as aptly describe De Quincey's own writing against the grain as 'the breviary of Romanticism'; but we can see now that *Confessions* looked beyond Romanticism to the Decadence, and even beyond that to Symbolism and Surrealism.[12]

The significance of *Confessions*, however, transcends autobiography and literary history, and the English Opium-Eater is more than his creator's alter ego and the quintessential Romantic. He is also, and above all else, the quintessential modern man, tortured by that vague longing for an elusive ideal; painfully conscious that his pleasures are finite, his needs infinite. 'Thus, in revising, or it might be said in re-writing the *Confessions* ... he greatly enlarged the work; but having done so, began to feel misgivings' (Wright, 24). A letter to his youngest daughter, Emily De Quincey (1833-1917), dated September/October 1856, shows the extent of those misgivings:

> To justify the enormous labour it has cost me, most certainly it *ought* to be improved. And yet, reviewing the volume as a *whole*,

---

[12]For example, in André Breton's surrealist novel, *Nadja* (1928), the narrator says: 'My image of the "ghost," including everything conventional about its appearance as well as its blind submission to certain contingencies of time and place, is particularly significant for me as the finite representation of a torment that may be eternal. Perhaps my life is nothing but an image of this kind; perhaps I am doomed to retrace my steps under the illusion that I am exploring, doomed to try and learn what I should simply recognize, learning a mere fraction of what I have forgotten. This sense of myself seems inadequate only insofar as it *presupposes* myself, arbitrarily preferring a completed image of my mind which need not be reconciled with time, and insofar as it implies – within the same time – an idea of irreparable loss, of punishment, of a fall whose lack of moral basis is, as I see it, indisputable.' (translated by Richard Howard, 12.)

now that I can look back from nearly the end to the beginning, greatly I doubt whether many readers will not prefer it in its original fragmentary state to its present full-blown development ... Here, again, as in thousands of similar cases, is a conflict – a call for a choice – between an almost *extempore* effort, having the faults, the carelessness, possibly the graces, of a fugitive imagination – this on the one side, and on the other a studied and mature presentation of the same thoughts, facts, and feelings, but without the same benefit from extemporaneous excitement.

– Morrison, 239

At the beginning of his writing career the tension between the business of autobiography and the nightmare of his own delinquencies gave his best work its tautness, and the crackle of 'extemporaneous excitement' was sent out as an urgent and affectionate greeting to souls in similar crises. Look at this early paragraph of the 1821 version:

I have often been asked, how I first came to be a regular opium-eater; and have suffered, very unjustly, in the opinion of my acquaintance, from being reputed to have brought upon myself all the sufferings which I shall have to record, by a long course of indulgence in this practice purely for the sake of creating an artificial state of pleasurable excitement. This, however, is a misrepresentation of my case.

– Morrison, 7

But during the 1820s, 30s, 40s and 50s that tension was loosened and lost in journalistic improvisation, padding and recycling, and the relentless need to provide editors with copy. Long-windedness would take over. Look at the 1856 version:

I have often been asked – how it was, and through what series of steps, that I became an opium-eater. Was it gradually, tentatively,

mistrustingly, as one goes down a shelving beach into a deepening
sea, and with a knowledge from the first of the dangers lying on
that path; half-courting those dangers, in fact, whilst seeming to
defy them? Or was it, secondly, in pure ignorance of such dangers,
under the misleading of mercenary fraud? Since oftentimes lozenges,
for the relief of pulmonary affections, found their efficacy upon
the opium which they contain, upon this, and this only, though
clamorously disavowing so suspicious an alliance: and under such
treacherous disguises, multitudes are seduced into a dependency
which they had not foreseen upon a day which they had not known:
not known even by name, or by sight: and thus the case is not rare
– that the chain of abject slavery is first detected when it has
inextricably wound itself about the constitutional system. Thirdly,
and lastly, was it [*Yes*, by passionate anticipation, I answer, before
the question is finished] – was it on a sudden, overmastering impulse
derived from bodily anguish? Loudly I repeat, *Yes*; loudly and
indignantly – as in answer to a wilful calumny.

– Milligan, xxii

The psychological acuity is still in the writing. One may remember
the feeling of lowering oneself down that 'shelving beach' from
innocence into deepening experience. But all the superfluous
phrases – ' ... oftentimes lozenges ... the misleading of mercenary
fraud ... ' – become too niggling, and merely *amusing*[13] whereas
the original publication in the autumn of 1821 had been an inspired
delight. Baudelaire didn't bother with the long-winded *Confessions*,
but rather based his translation entirely on the original version, to
which he added sections of *Suspiria*. He saw at once that the original
book epitomised the spiritual anguish of modern times.

---

[13]De Quincey himself worried, in 1856: 'as a book of *amusement* it is
undoubtedly improved; what I doubt is, whether it is a book to *impress* ... '
(Morrison, 239)

Coleridge had read the original *Confessions* with 'unutterable sorrow ... The writer with morbid vanity, makes a boast of what was my misfortune.' (Morrison, *English Opium Eater*, 211) Thankfully for De Quincey, Coleridge wasn't around to hold forth on the problems of the later *Confessions*. Behind De Quincey's addiction and his futile efforts to conquer it, there is a spiritual affliction which does even more to exalt his autobiographical work than his considerable talent. His supreme achievement was to have created, out of an extraordinary figure (himself, modelled on Coleridge), a type, representative not simply of a group, or of a generation, or even just of the nineteenth century, but of an entire epoch that has lasted through to today.

22 ♦ Anecdotes for Mother

'Listen carefully to first criticisms of your work. Note carefully just what it is about your work that the critics don't like – then cultivate it. That's the part of your work that's individual and worth keeping ... '

– Jean Cocteau

To young De Quincey, the mythology and poetry shared by the Coleridge-Wordsworth circle provided a spacious habitation for his contemplative – and even morbid – temperament. In the Coleridge-Wordsworth circle, rich and deep experiences shared by all were expressed and evoked. Here, convicts, exiles, idiot boys and female vagrants were understood. Here, dogmatism, institutionalism and the wretched sciences of place-hunting and cronyism would surely be eschewed. Here, therefore, was where

De Quincey, at fifteen, decided he wanted to be. Staying with his mother, or going where his mother wanted to send him, was out of the question.

De Quincey and his mother had an understanding that needed few words. But he was an exceptionally bright boy who learned how to use lots of words. The more words he would use to his mother to explain his way out of a tight situation (such as when he tried to persuade her not to send him to Manchester Grammar School, or when he tried – as he would many times throughout her long life – to get more money out of her), the less precisely she would seem to listen to him, and the more she would seem to see through the words to the wily, panicky, slippery, inky-fingered son generating them like an uncooperative cuttlefish. She was usually keen to detect the ulterior motive, or anything else lurking and needing corrected or eliminated. In this respect, Wordsworth's 'Anecdote for Fathers; Shewing How the Art of Lying Might be Taught' was instructive for De Quincey. In the poem, the adult is overbearing in conversation with the young child and obliges him to answer his boring and irrelevant question.

> 'My little boy, which like you more,'
> I said and took him by the arm –
> 'Our home by Kilve's delightful shore,
> 'Or here at Liswyn farm?'
>
> 'And tell me, had you rather be,'
> I said and held him by the arm,
> 'At Kilve's smooth shore by the green sea,
> 'Or here at Liswyn farm?'

Kilve or Liswyn? The boy is compelled by the adult to answer one

way or the other. He doesn't at first, but then he realises that he
has no choice, so he does what many children (and adults,
including, for that matter, members of the voting public) do when
coerced into binary – he gives any old answer:

> In careless mood he looked at me,
> While still I held him by the arm,
> And said, 'At Kilve I'd rather be
> 'Than here at Liswyn farm.'

> 'Now, little Edward, say why so;
> My little Edward, tell me why;'
> 'I cannot tell, I do not know,'
> 'Why this is strange,' said I.

But any old answer just won't do for the speaker, who argues the
other way, as if he is an illustrious builder of boys' characters,
eminently able to teach by example the discipline of reasoning:

> 'For, here are woods and green-hills warm;
> 'There surely must some reason be
> 'Why you would change sweet Liswyn farm
> 'For Kilve by the green sea.'

> At this, my boy, so fair and slim,
> Hung down his head, nor made reply;
> And five times did I say to him,
> 'Why? Edward, tell me why?'

Forced into being more ostentatiously involved in the uninteresting
discussion, the exposed and uncomfortable (but spirited) boy finds
a way to draw the matter short. As if justly reaching over some
shadow-line separating resourcefulness and disingenuousness, he

gets hold of what he needs and delivers to his interrogator an answer with a 'reason' attached.

> His head he raised – there was in sight,
> It caught his eye, he saw it plain –
> Upon the house-top, glittering bright,
> A broad and gilded vane.

> Then did the boy his tongue unlock,
> And thus to me he made reply;
> 'At Kilve there was no weather-cock,
> 'And that's the reason why.'

Lies like this are not such stuff as dreams are made on. Sadly, such lies must routinely be generated in response to petty tyrants and unimaginative people. They are the outcome of everyday oppression, and even of the whole spectrum of oppression from the merely thwarting and obstinate ways of De Quincey's guardian (Rev Samuel Hall) all the way up to the deadly reasoning of Robespierre and his Committee of Public Safety. As John F. Danby has put it, the speaker of Wordsworth's 'Anecdote for Fathers' has apparently stepped 'out of the frame of mere "literature" altogether and into the reader's own reality' (*The Simple Wordsworth*, 1960, 38) – the reality of relations analogically lived and felt rather than logically accounted for. De Quincey, the runaway, the outsider, the hole-in-the-corner man, learned to live between the lines of this poetry.

23 ◆ Writing Home, and Writing Involutes

At those times in his life when he communicated with his mother exclusively by post, he would be conscious of having an advantage: when his mother had no Thomas actually present upon whom to focus in person, he would find himself free to open up as he wished, in equilibrium with the brighter, better new world of the *Lyrical Ballads*. Rising to a fuller and more real stature in the realm of ink and paper, he found that he could get some leverage with his mother that he had been unable to get with her in person.

He found also that he was freer to see how close his unsolicited effusions could get him to his hero, Wordsworth:

> ... though you may find many minds more congenial with your own, and therefore more proportionately more worthy of your regard, you will never find any one more zealously attached to you – more full of admiration for your mental excellence and of reverential love for your moral character – more ready (I speak from my heart!) to sacrifice even his life – whenever it could have a chance of promoting your interest and happiness – than he who now bends the knee before you.
>
> – Wright, 386-87

But the shadows – the depths of bewilderment, desire and despair in which he had been buffeted as a child and schoolboy, and from which he for a time thought he could liberate himself in the actual company of the poets whose works had changed his life – would regather. Despite De Quincey finally making it into Wordsworth's family circle, and even into his employ, the shadowy energies would always regather, and the depths would always sigh, drawing him back to the roots of his being, verticalizing his whole life by a fleeting sensation. For example, 'the sun of midsummer ... showering down torrents of splendour' would forever be bound up in his imagination with the sight of the dead body of his sister Elizabeth (Morrison, 96). Like Frankenstein's monster, or like the brooding Byronic fugitive, he could at any moment suddenly be convulsed into subjection to the vitality of the events that had brought him into being and shaped him:

> But ever and anon of griefs subdued
> There comes a token like a scorpion's sting,
> Scarce seen, but with fresh bitterness imbued;
> And slight withal may be the things which bring
> Back on the heart the weight which it would fling
> Aside for ever: it may be a sound –
> A tone of music – summer's eve – or spring –
> A flower – the wind – the ocean – which shall wound,
> Striking the electric chain wherewith we are darkly bound.
>
> – Byron, *Childe Harold's Pilgrimage*, Canto IV, xxiv

Like Byron, and like Coleridge, De Quincey could be connected by the recollection of a place, event or circumstance to another place and another time:

> O Heaven when I think how perishable Things, how imperishable Thoughts seem to be! - for what is Forgetfulness? Renew the state of affection or bodily Feeling [...] and instantly the trains of forgotten Thought rise from their living catacombs!—Old men, & Infancy/and Opium, probably by its narcotic effect[...] produces the same effect on the visual, & passive memory ...
>
> – *Coleridge Notebook*, I, 1575

The amount De Quincey had changed in the recognition of such a moment was what he called the involute (Morrison, 97) – the path he had followed to reach the same point on another winding. Every experience of an individual human being has the potential to fuse with every other experience to haunt that individual. Memories of situations recur with increasing familiarity until the individual masters or entangles them in the light of the previous time round:

> ... far more of our deepest thoughts and feelings pass to us through perplexed combinations of *concrete* objects, pass to us as *involutes* (if I may coin that word) in compound experiences incapable of being disentangled, than ever reach us *directly* in their own shapes.
>   – Morrison, 97[14]

The involute he travels round life is the means he has to compare himself with himself, and the means with which he may discover how much he has changed since he was last in, say, Manchester, or Everton, or London, or the last time he saw his favourite sister alive, or dead. Time itself might be cyclical, and this might be why the involutes of its returning memories, moods or seasons mean that the writer can review the growth of his understanding:

> The reader must suppose me at Oxford: twelve years and a half are gone by; I am in the glory of youthful happiness; but I have now first tampered with opium; and now first the agitations of my childhood reopened in strength, now first they swept in upon the brain with power and the grandeur of recovered life, under the separate and the concurring inspirations of opium.
> Once again, after twelve years' interval, the nursery of my childhood expanded before me – my sister was moaning in bed – I

---

[14]'De Quincey's "involutes" are strikingly similar to Wordsworth's "spots of time", for both concepts are rooted in childhood memory, and involve emotions and material objects that have become inextricably combined.' (Morrison, 296)

> was beginning to be restless with fears not intelligible to myself.
> Once again the nurse, but now dilated to colossal proportions ...
> smote me senseless to the ground. Again, I was in the chamber
> with my sister's corpse – again the pomps of life rose up in silence,
> the glory of summer, the frost of death. Dream formed itself
> mysteriously within dream; within these Oxford dreams remoulded
> itself continually the trance in my sister's chamber, – the blue
> heavens, the everlasting vault, the soaring billows ... Once more the
> funeral procession gathered ...
>
>   – Morrison, 129-30

De Quincey's autobiographical writing was effectively the involute
house he built to keep him from life's incessant outpouring, from
an otherwise unrestricted flow into the dark, into death itself. Since
what is unknown has power over us, we should otherwise be as
defenceless as the mollusc would be if its shell grew long and
straight. (De Quincey found the word 'involute' in conchology.)
The familiarity of life's experience is the mind's way of winding
itself around and sheltering itself, creating those mysterious
vantage-points, glimpses of half-hidden windings which vivify
consciousness as it speculates and anticipates. (Jill Purce, *Journey
of the Soul*, 7)

    For De Quincey, unveiled truth and death could well be the
same thing. As John Beer has said, De Quincey 'was particularly
impressed by the account of an old lady concerning what had
happened to her when she almost drowned at the age of nine'
(Beer, *Romantic Consciousness*, 90):

> At a certain stage of this descent, a blow seemed to strike her –
> phosphoric radiance sprang forth from her eyeballs; and
> immediately a mighty theatre expanded within her brain. In a
> moment, in the twinkling of an eye, every act – every design of her

past life, lived again – arraying themselves not as succession, but as parts of a coexistence. Such a light fell upon the whole path of her life backwards into the shades of infancy, as the light perhaps which wrapt the destined apostle on his road to Damascus. Yet that light blinded for a season; but hers poured celestial vision upon the brain, so that her consciousness became omnipresent at one moment to every feature in the infinite review.

– Morrison, 136-7

24 ◆ The Convention of Dreamers

The twenty-two-year-old De Quincey was hired by Wordsworth in 1808 to get his political pamphlet *The Convention of Cintra* – in which Wordsworth criticised the agreement made between the French, British, and Portuguese during the Peninsular War (1808–14) – ready for the press. But there was something about the way De Quincey was going about things that kept his new father-figure – for that was what Wordsworth had, by 1808, in a sense become – cagey, crabbed and on his case.

It was a trying, and perhaps defining, time in De Quincey's young adult life, during which he found out what it felt like to not know exactly what duties he was expected to be discharging in the workplace: Wordsworth seems to have seen him as something of a functionary, mostly a mere messenger between poet-pamphleteer and printer; De Quincey had a rather infirm self-image of a proper editor with authority to get involved intellectually. The petty stress of this unsure arrangement was compounded by the conduct of the printers, who often got drunk. There were many large errors, and De Quincey had to get a new compositor. Perhaps with more worldly skill in, say, parrying queries and repackaging the undesirable results of incompetent co-workers' habits, he might have better contained any breaking news of the practical problems and just got on with delivering an excellent finished product. But he didn't, and Wordsworth thought, frankly, that there was something shiftless in his new friend and acolyte. De Quincey saw that Wordsworth thought as much. Their fondness for one another began to fade.

To make matters worse, Wordsworth then began to worry that the pamphlet might contain, or even constitute, a libel. It was, after all, an expression of indignation at Britain's treaty with the enemy (France) which meant that French troops and their loot could be taken from Portugal back to France in British ships. Wordsworth made last-minute requests for De Quincey to make some rather awkward surgical changes. This led to further annoyance and confusion, and further delays.

De Quincey's system of punctuation seemed to be emerging as symptomatic of some central inadequacy, or even delinquency. Coleridge said De Quincey's 'strange & most mistaken System of punctuation' had damaged *Cintra*'s readability: 'Never was a stranger whim than the notion that , ; : and . could be made logical symbols expressing all the diversities of logical connection.' (*Coleridge Letters*, III, 214) Wordsworth's Cintra/De Quincey debacle had become the talk of the literary Lakers. Robert Southey told Walter Scott that Wordsworth's 'long and involved sentences' had been rendered 'more obscure' by De Quincey's 'unusual system of punctuation' (Morrison, *English Opium Eater*, 140-46).

Now, Wordsworth's little helper was a bit too perplexingly like Wordsworth's little cottage girl in 'We Are Seven', but with the difference that the little girl turned out to have something to offer in the shape of a poet's food for thought. Not so with the eccentric man-child, who was becoming, in Margaret Russett's phrase, 'the personification of *material* resistance to the philosophic mind.' (Russett, *De Quincey's Romanticism: Canonical Minority and the Forms of Transmission*, 87) 'Twas throwing words away.

De Quincey was one of those people one can never be sure *really* doesn't know some of the very basic things he needs to know but *seems* not to. In other words, De Quincey was infuriating. If the little cottage girl's mysterious mode of wisdom was, finally, not lost on the speaker of 'We Are Seven', the little poppy man's mode of helpfulness was, usually, lost on Wordsworth.

Perhaps this was because by the time Wordsworth met De Quincey, the former no longer believed – as he once did in the mid-1790s with the exciting and mystical young Coleridge – that everything in nature (including human nature) hangs together in the deepest sense. If Coleridge found the lovely shapes and sounds of nature 'intelligible', by the late 1790s Wordsworth found himself finding nature *un*intelligible. Having heard, say, the strange utterances of the loud dry wind, or having felt a presence that disturbed him with the joy of elevated thoughts, he would find himself left with what he called 'the burthen of the mystery'. Nature seemed to be speaking a language he could not understand, puzzle over it as he might. It was even rather a frightening idiom:

> my brain
> Work'd with a dim and undetermin'd sense
> Of unknown modes of being; in my thoughts
> There was a darkness, call it solitude,
> Or blank desertion, no familiar shapes

> Of hourly objects, images of trees,
> Of sea or sky, no colours of green fields;
> But huge and mighty Forms that do not live
> Like living men mov'd slowly through the mind
> By day and were the trouble of my dreams.

— *The Prelude*, I

Nature had taken his father from him. (His father had lost his way home on the moors and had to spend the night there, which resulted in his death from hypothermia.) Nature was something of a savage god that could send searching experiences far into the heart of a growing boy: at one moment moonlit lake water might be lapping around your little boat, and the next moment one of the huge surrounding shapes in the dark might suddenly seem to *get up* and give chase – striding after you like one of Milton's devils.

> When from behind that craggy Steep, till then
> The bound of the horizon, a huge Cliff,
> As if with voluntary power instinct,
> Uprear'd its head. I struck, and struck again
> And, growing still in stature, the huge Cliff
> Rose up between me and the stars, and still,
> With measur'd motion, like a living thing,
> Strode after me.

— *The Prelude*, I

Your guilty conscience (perhaps you have 'stolen' the boat) seems to have something to do with it, but that sort of thing will be for the psychologists to sort out a century later. In the meantime, you yourself are caught in the toils. As Kathleen Raine has put it, Wordsworth

... was not recording his individual experiences because they were unique but because they were universal. He assumed the role of Everyman, because it is through the uniqueness of the individual self through whose mediation alone we perceive the world, singular to each yet common to all. This role he took on, in this sense, to explore his own particular ego, in the name of anonymity. The eye of universal consciousness receives only in the particular life what is our universal heritage.

– Raine, *That Wondrous Pattern*, 217

Wordsworth could show the insides of humans in a way that they had not been shown before. He was the spiritual guide of his time in England. His house was plain, even shabby, though it did not seem so to De Quincey, but rather had the air of a house whose chairs, children, curtains, tables and plants were all special occupants, like a group of old friends, well-born though modest. Any disliked person or thing, any guest or resident, could no more have been banished than the creatures from the Creation. 'Let the wheat and the weeds grow together until the harvest.' (Matthew 13:30)

De Quincey felt the freshness and force of the Wordsworthian energies coursing through the writing and the living alike. But he found that he could do nothing to add to or assist the enterprise. He could only be a taker and not a giver in this circle. He could never freshen and revitalise here, only poison and weaken. Wordsworth's work was what it was because all of a piece, his values, his people, including his wife and sister, and his friend Coleridge, from whom he learned so much (yet still had authority over), down through all the minutiae of the plain living behind the high thinking – the family's readings aloud from the works of Spenser, Milton and Shakespeare, their discussions of books, their wanderings in the countryside, Dorothy's collecting wild thyme, foxgloves, ferns, primroses, bluebells and columbine, her sowing of peas, turnips, radishes, broccoli, bistort and runner beans, the honeysuckle, sweet peas and roses that covered the cottage's walls, her journals – with those observations of the natural world that so inspired her brother into poetic utterance ...

De Quincey knew he would never really have the beauty of what was made in the Wordsworth circle. He knew that no parasite can inherit the bee's knowledge or the secret of its honey.

25 ♦ The Convention of Guilty Consciences

If as a child growing up in the Lake District you felt guilty about stealing little rowing boats, or birds' eggs, you might go on to feel even more guilty about leaving your French lover and your illegitimate child to fend for themselves in Terror-stricken France. Back in England, you might feel the settling misery of this guilt as the months and years go by without your being able or willing to return to France. Little wonder then if the company and conversation of a solitary little cottage girl in a churchyard pressurises you into poetry. Little wonder too that you will look to your gifted and charismatic new friend, Coleridge, for fantastic responses to life's big questions. Joining forces with that 'wonderful man', as Dorothy called Coleridge, and engaging with life's big questions rather than engaging with your own problems is displacement activity – another thing (a 'coping mechanism') for the psychologists to unveil in the twentieth century. And no wonder you will write your life down in a way that you can handle – and no wonder you will surround yourself as you do this with women (sister Dorothy, wife Mary) who adore and believe in you.

Although Wordsworth is very quotable (for example, his espousal of 'plain living and high thinking'), he resists brief summary. Colin Burrow has put it nicely: '[Wordsworth's] particular genius is to make you believe things without really telling you what they are.' ('A Solemn and Unsexual Man', *London Review of Books*, 4 July 2019) Even sympathetic readers have seen him as an enigma or contradiction, struggling to understand (for example) how he could see poetry as 'a spontaneous overflow of powerful emotions' *and* 'strong emotion recollected in tranquillity'. Perhaps part of what made him unassailable was that his most sustained and profound piece, *The Prelude*, was unseen by the public until the year of his death, 1850. Until then, the poem existed in manuscript form only, and was read or heard recited by very few. One of the few was Coleridge, who heard Wordsworth recite it in 1807. The impact was so strong for Coleridge that he felt like a drowning man who has been swept to safety – only to find himself swept back to a familiar state of emergency about which he knew too well he could do nothing for himself:

> Ah! as I listened with a heart forlorn,
> The pulses of my being beat anew:
> And even as Life returns upon the drowned,
> Life's joy rekindling roused a throng of pains
> > – 'To William Wordsworth'

Wordsworth – who wrote poetry so radiant and captivating – seemed yet somehow to have something about him inhospitable to the very souls finding themselves attracted to him. (Colin Burrow has said that 'Wordsworth was the first poet I fell in love with as a teenager.') For example, the following passage evokes – or perhaps invokes – a boy undergoing a formative experience, but from an earlier draft it is clear that the boy was in fact the poet ('I', not 'he') himself. Wordsworth needed to put himself at a further remove from the reader in order to invest the poetry with more of a sense of the arrival of wisdom from some special elsewhere – almost as if it had been uttered by the hills and clouds themselves:

> There was a Boy; ye knew him well, ye cliffs
> And islands of Winander! ...
> ... sometimes, in that silence, while he hung
> Listening, a gentle shock of mild surprise
> Has carried far into his heart the voice
> Of mountain-torrents; or the visible scene
> Would enter unawares into his mind
> With all its solemn imagery, its rocks,
> Its woods, and that uncertain heaven received
> Into the bosom of the steady lake.
>
> – *The Prelude*, I

Wordsworth's 'heaven' is the sky, presumably with clouds in it, seen reflected in the water rather than directly – hence it is as much a foreshadowing of psychology as it is an intimation of immortality. All the scenery is perfectly natural and believable. The poem seems to want to cater for both the mystically and secularly inclined.

Coleridge had fantasised about reviving in its totality the 'symphony and song' of his dream of paradise. He had imagined dreaming of paradise, plucking a flower in that dream, and waking from the dream with the flower in his hand. He had patrolled the grey area between consciousness and unconsciousness, and attempted to examine the precise nature of each by separating them, and superimposing one on the other:

> Frid. Morn. 5 o'clock – Dosing, dreamt of Hartley as at his Christening – how as he was asked who redeemed him, & was to say, God the Son/he went on humming and hawing, in one hum & haw, like a boy who knows a thing & will not make the effort to recollect it – so as to irritate me greatly. Awakening gradually I was able compleately to detect, that it was the Ticking of my Watch which lay in the Pen Place in my Desk on the round Table close by my Ear, & which in the diseased State of my Nerves had *fretted* on my Ears – I caught the fact while Hartley's Face & moving Lips were yet before my Eyes, & his Hum & Ha, & the Ticking of the Watch were each the other, as often happens in the passing off of Sleep – that curious modification of Ideas by each other ... I arose instantly, & wrote it down – it is now 10 minutes past 5.
>
> *– Notebook* 1, 1620

Just as the crawling chaos of nightmare monsters will linger for De Quincey even in the orderly domestic sight of his children standing at his bedside, so Coleridge's sleeping and waking lives mingle into something unique which is experienced right up against the limits of consciousness. With Coleridge and De Quincey there is often this sense of the scientifically experimental occasion – or the performance of alchemy.

Wordsworth had modernised himself on his own, and he was (in 'There was a Boy', quoted above) able to show a heaven that (exchanged and received as it is in the natural and human worlds) doubtless exists – but is *uncertain*. This is the very heaven perhaps best cherished in the *steady* bosom rather than blabbered about by damaged or opium-addled archangels. Coleridge perceived that what Wordsworth had to teach had come 'From the dread watchtower of man's absolute self' ('To William Wordsworth') – and said that if he had ever seen the lines 'that uncertain heaven received/Into the bosom of the steady lake' drop out of the clear blue sky when he was walking alone through an Arabian desert, he would instantly have screamed out 'Wordsworth!' (Beer, *Romantic Consciousness*, 94).

Like Poe's Raven, or Frankenstein's monster, or the Ancient Mariner (or the man who invented him), De Quincey, the teenage runaway in transports of admiration for Wordsworth and Coleridge, has only to see their mountains to bring them low, or drink their waters to make them bitter, or tread their rocks to make them barren, or find their Lakes to make them lost. That is what tourism – even *spiritual* tourism – so often does. Upon the door of Dove Cottage, De Quincey's shadow fell, and he caused distrust, and later distress. Just as the Raven can croak 'Nevermore' with dismaying regularity, so might it be again re-echoed that we are all De Quinceyan now.

26 ◆ *Habituated to the Vast*

> For thou wert there, thine own brows garlanded,
> Amid the tremor of a realm aglow,
> Amid the mighty nation jubilant,
> When from the general heart of human kind
> Hope sprang forth like a full-born Deity!
>
> – 'To William Wordsworth'

De Quincey would join Coleridge in what amounted to a sort of worship of Wordsworth from a distance. Coleridge and De Quincey would see themselves as uniquely equipped to recognise and deliver Wordsworth's genius to the public. If De Quincey's father figure was Wordsworth, this father was now absent, and De Quincey sought the comfort and company of a brother figure instead. Coleridge was, like De Quincey, devoted to the case of promoting himself via Wordsworth (Burwick, 34) and *habituated to the Vast* via opium. Coleridge wished to float like the Indian Vishnu, 'along an infinite ocean cradled in the flower of the Lotos, & wake once in a million years for a few minutes – just to know that I was going to sleep a million years more.' He felt the need to remain open. 'I can at times feel strongly the beauties, you describe, in themselves, & for themselves', as he told John Thelwall in 1797,

> but more frequently all things appear little – all the knowledge, that can be acquired, child's play – the universe itself – what but an immense heap of little things? – I can contemplate nothing but parts, & parts are all little – ! – My mind feels as if it ached to behold & know something great – something one & indivisible – and it is only in the faith of this that rocks or waterfalls, mountains or caverns give me the sense of sublimity or majesty!

As Hazlitt put it:

> Mr Coleridge is too rich in intellectual wealth, to need to task himself to any drudgery: he has only to draw the sliders of his imagination, and a thousand subjects expand before him, startling him with their brilliancy, or losing themselves in endless obscurity.

Coleridge grew old with his own magical – and, crucially, unfinished – poems and projects:

> There [at the Inner Temple, London] Coleridge sometimes ... took his seat; and then the genial hubbub of voices was still; critics,

philosophers, and poets, were contented to listen; and toil-worn lawyers, clerks from the India House, and members of the Stock Exchange, grew romantic while he spoke. Lamb used to say that he was inferior then to what he had been in his youth; but I can scarcely believe it; at least there is nothing in his early writing which gives any idea of the richness of his mind so lavishly poured out at this time in his happiest moods. Although he looked much older than he was, his hair being silvered all over, and his person tending to corpulency, there was about him no trace of bodily sickness or mental decay, but rather an air of voluptuous repose. His benignity of manner placed his auditors entirely at their ease; and inclined them to listen delighted to the sweet, low tone in which he began to discourse on some high theme. Whether he has won for his greedy listener only some raw lad, or charmed a circle of beauty, rank and wit, who hung breathless on his words, he talked with equal eloquence; for his subject, not his audience, inspired him. At first his tones were conversational; he seemed to dally with the shadows of the subject and with fantastic images which bordered it: but gradually the thought grew deeper, and the voice deepened with the thought; the stream gathering strength, seemed to bear along with it all things which opposed its progress, and blended them with its current; and stretching away among regions tinted with ethereal colours, was lost at airy distance in the horizon of fancy. His hearers were unable to grasp his theories, which were indeed too vast to be exhibited in the longest conversation; but they perceived noble images, generous suggestions, affecting pictures of virtue, which enriched their minds and nurtured their best affections. Coleridge was sometimes induced to recite portions of 'Christabel', then enshrined in manuscript from eyes profane, and gave a bewitching effect to its wizard lines. But more peculiar in its beauty than this, was his recitation of Kubla Khan. As he repeated the passage –

A damsel with a dulcimer
In a vision once I saw:

> It was an Abyssinian maid,
> And on her dulcimer she played,
> Singing of Mont Abora!

his voice seemed to mount and melt into air, as the images grew more visionary, and the suggested associations more remote.
– *The Works of Charles Lamb, with A Sketch of His Life by Sir Thomas Noon Talfourd* vol. 1, 1855, 260-1

Those who heard him talk were often dazzled, and yet more often they would not remember the actual topics Coleridge touched upon. His genius seemed to require, if not outright vagueness, then a certain lack of traction in daylight reality. So did De Quincey's. But, as Mike Jay has put it, 'By blaming opium for the human condition, Coleridge had become its martyr; by confessing what his mentor could not, De Quincey would become its Pope.' ('The Pope of Opium')

Wordsworth can tell you that the voice of mountain torrents has carried far into the heart of a growing boy. He doesn't, however, tell you how. He doesn't even explain if this voice carried itself or was carried somehow. And he doesn't tell you that the boy was himself. (Remember the 'I' became 'he' after the first draft, and with that sleight of the poet's hand, he disappeared himself into his art.) As Hazlitt put it,

The current of his feelings is deep, but narrow; the range of his understanding is lofty and aspiring rather than discursive. The force, the originality, the absolute truth and identity with which he feels some things, makes him indifferent to so many others.
– 'Mr Wordsworth', *Spirit of the Age*

27 ◆ Hard task to analyse a soul

Rather like the postman you irrationally yet dearly love for merely leaving you the package, Wordsworth delivers and is gone, and you are left to unwrap, puzzle over and take pleasure in the contents without any further assistance. He doesn't seem to hang around in a manner as anxiously solicitous as Coleridge. Wordsworth, conscious since his youth, as he told Isabella Fenwick in 1843, 'of the infinite variety of natural appearances which had been unnoticed by the poets of any age or country', organised himself in accordance with supply and demand, and 'made a resolution to supply in some degree the deficiency.'

Coleridge, less determined, says he cares not from whose mouth Truth comes – as long as it is Truth. Hence, nothing that Coleridge says can be taken automatically as his own invention. Norman Fruman has comprehensively demolished Coleridge as an original thinker. Since the publication of Fruman's *Coleridge: The Damaged Archangel* in 1972, Coleridge enthusiasts have had to rethink what there actually is in Coleridge to be so enthusiastic about. However, circulating still in the economy of English literature are the Cumbrian lakes, hills, clouds, cliffs and islands – and all as if with the Wordsworthian watermark. Wordsworth doesn't get bogged down in metaphysics (or metaphysicians' lucubrations):

> But who shall parcel out
> His intellect, by geometric rules,
> Split, like a province, into round and square?
> Who knows the individual hour in which
> His habits were first sown, even as a seed,
> Who that shall point, as with a wand, and say,
> 'This portion of the river of my mind
> Came from yon fountain?' ...

Hard task to analyse a soul, in which,
Not only general habits and desires,
But each most obvious and particular thought,
Not in a mystical and idle sense,
But in the words of reason deeply weigh'd,
Hath no beginning.

– *The Prelude*, I

His 'this' and 'yon' and so on lend a crucial lightness of touch to his handling of the ideas of philosophers (such as, here, probably, John Locke) who conceive of themselves merely in terms of mechanistic science. Wordsworth can offer the word 'soul' in a way that may be taken up by a reader as something (such as a 'self') altogether more secular and low maintenance than a machine with a ghost in it. In a way, Wordsworth could preserve in his writing an atmosphere propitious to a sense of wonder, yet without having to be at hopeless loggerheads with the obdurate materialism of the age. Rather than propose a friendship, a love (the ready rush of sympathy, the atmosphere of love in which ideas might be most powerfully exchanged and received), Wordsworth provided a *service*. It was his way of pulling up the drawbridge – or putting his hands in his britches pockets, as Keats put it – without priggishly declaring his position as ultimately superior. He just wanted to get on with his high thinking. The oracle of the modern era had arrived under the flag of helpfulness. He said in a letter to De Quincey that he was sure 'from the interest you have taken in the L.B. [*Lyrical Ballads*] that it [*The Prelude*] would please you, and might be of service to you.'

It certainly was. But instead of showing its most fanatical reader how to live, it incited him to open to the public the 'theatre' of his own brain. Hard task to analyse a soul? If Wordsworth had attempted it by looking in 'hiding places ten years deep', De Quincey had his way of penetrating through to the regions of the soul where the monstrous vegetations of the sick mind flourish.[15]

> I too deeply recognize the mind affected by my morbid condition ... [Coleridge's] chaos I comprehended by the darkness of my own, and both were the work of laudanum. It was as if ivory carving and elaborate fretwork and fair enameling should be found with worms and ashes amongst coffins and the wrecks of some forgotten life or some abolished nature. In parts and fractions eternal creations are carried on, but the nexus is wanting, and life and the central principle which should bind together all the parts at the centre, with all its radiations to the circumference, are wanting. Infinite incoherence, ropes of sand, gloomy incapacity of vital pervasions by some one plastic principle, that is the hideous incubus upon my mind always.
> – Japp, *Thomas De Quincey: His Life and Writings*, I, 340

Perhaps De Quincey recognised this condition when he read Coleridge's letter from 'a friend' at the end of Chapter 13 of the *Biographia Literaria*. (If Wordsworth had recollected strong emotion in tranquillity, Coleridge was forgetting strong philosophical exertion at the request of his imaginary friend.)

The 'friend' (really, Coleridge) suggested in the letter that Coleridge was a ruin, and he was always being pulled downward – his was the melancholy logic, the subtlety of decay, and he moved further into his soft evening of ashes:

---

[15]When Maria Edgeworth read Milton's lines about Hell ('And in the lowest deep a lower deep / Still threatening to devour me opens wide'), she objected. How could the lowest deep open into a lower deep? De Quincey answered, 'In carpentry, it is clear to my mind that it could *not*.' But in cases of 'deep imaginative feeling' it was natural to behold the 'never-ending growth of one colossal grandeur chasing and surmounting another, or of abysses that swallowed up abysses.'

> A grief without a pang, void, dark, and drear,
> A stifled, drowsy, unimpassioned grief,
> Which finds no natural outlet, no relief,
>   In word, or sigh, or tear
> > — Coleridge, 'Dejection: An Ode'

As T.S. Eliot would say, the ruined man would be a vocation in itself. It was, also, after all, Benjamin Disraeli's vocation as a young man, long before he un-ruined himself to become the Prime Minister.[16]

28 ◆ The Friend

De Quincey, too, would include in his self-dramatization, *Confessions*, a friend (Ann, the prostitute) whose actual existence cannot be proved because there is no record or recollection of her anywhere other than in De Quincey's account. Similarly, the

---

[16]'At present I indulge only in a calm reverie, for I find the least exertion of mind instantly aggravates all my symptoms , and even this letter is an exertion which you wo[ul]d hardly credit. But to exist, and to feel existence more tolerable, to observe, and to remember, to record a thought that suddenly starts up, or catch a new image which glances over the surface of my mind – this is still left me. But the moment that I attempt to meditate or combine, to ascertain a question that is doubtful or in anyway to call the greatest powers of intellect into play, that moment I feel I am a lost man. The palpitation in my heart and head increases in violence, an indescribable feeling of idiocy comes over me, and for hours I am plunged in a state of the darkest despair. When the curse has subsided to its usual grade of horror, my sanguine temper calls me again to life and hope.' (W.A. Speck, 'Byron and Disraeli: The Mediterranean Tours', *The Wordsworth Circle*, XLIII, 2, Spring 2012, 106-113, 109)

existence of the person on business from Porlock – first mentioned in a Preface written twenty years after the poem itself was first written, offering an intellectual justification for *Kubla Khan*'s lack of completion – is unprovable. The reader must either take the author's word for it or not. Or, to speak the language of Coleridge's self-sustaining sphere, the reader may willingly suspend his or her disbelief. Hence, there can be a sense that the visionary bubble of the literary life could only (though so easily) be burst with a fact or two from some churlish and unimaginative enemy of poetry and poetic dreams ('A truth that's told with bad intent/Beats all the lies you can invent', as Blake had put it); some philistine with no spiritual hunger who thinks that merely to feed the body and educate the young for the performance of practical skills in the service of the profit motive is all there is; some agent of corruption and destruction who oversees the reductionism, profanation and trivialization which inevitably follows from a denial of vision ...

De Quincey, the self-elected interpreter (Burwick, 34) of Wordsworth, even 'amidst a wilderness of chattering buffoons' (Wright, 147), is also the villainous gutter-journalist not looking at the stars. As Stephen Gill has said, 'Observant, shrewd, by and large generous, De Quincey's essays are fascinating, but they broadcast exactly the kind of domestic detail that Wordsworth regarded as sacredly private.' (Gill, *William Wordsworth: A Life*, 387-88). Henry Crabb Robinson 'found De Quincey's Lake Reminiscences "scandalous but painfully interesting" (Henry Crabb Robinson, *On Books and Their Authors*, 1:273) – an achievement as biographer which De Quincey deliberately crafted and executed.' (Burwick, 42) At one point, De Quincey will point out Wordsworth's ability to deliver the reader the whole world as if through a re-enactment of the formative inrush of sensations (Burwick, 154-5); at another point, he will disclose 'a narrowness and a droop about [Wordsworth's] shoulders which ... had an effect of meanness when brought into close juxtaposition with a figure of a most statuesque order.' (Wright, 135) Here, he will remember that 'a light radiating from some far spiritual world' (Wright, 139) seemed to shine from Wordsworth's eyes; there, he will remember how Wordsworth was mistaken for a sixty-year-old when he was only thirty-eight (Wright, 142).

De Quincey tells his readers that 'Wordsworth is peculiarly the poet for the solitary and the meditative', but he can also deftly provide a context (as Coleridge deftly framed his ruin *Kubla Khan* with a Preface) in which the poet's sloping shoulders and premature ageing can be read about with pleasure less guilty: 'Commensurate with the interest in the poetry will be a secondary interest in the poet – in his personal appearance, and his habits of life, *so far as they can be supposed at all dependent upon his intellectual characteristics*' (Wright, 144-45).

In other words, when it comes to justifying the ways of genius to magazine-reading man, it takes one to know one. De Quincey showed readers that there *were* some *understandable* reasons for the neglect of Wordsworth, and that Wordsworth's story (like Hamlet's, Coleridge's and De Quincey's) is as much one of intellect and imagination as of actual achievement.

Coleridge's thought is multifarious and scattered across a vast array of writings, from which it must be quarried by the only scholar qualified to do this: De Quincey. De Quincey showed readers that Wordsworth was a master of poetry, but also that he remained somewhat alienated from his contemporaries in part because in his *Lyrical Ballads* he was decidedly *not* an apologist for aristocracy and privilege, and so perhaps a victim of the distaste that self-containment, self-assurance and reticence often inspire. His writings and even his letters are notably short on confidence, gossip or personal colour. This would become something far removed from the new confessional style – *The Confessions of J. Lackington* (1804), *The Confessions of William Henry Ireland* (1805), Charles Lamb's 'Confessions of a Drunkard' (1813) – in which 'De Quincey figures as a noble explorer of the self' (Morrison, *English Opium Eater*, 208).

29 ◆ Confessions of an English Poetry-Reader

Despite the sophisticated elegance of De Quincey at his best – his recollections and interpretations of the Lake poets and his own life – his writing remains somehow insular. Yes, his empathy with the poets is informed by his exhaustive knowledge of their huge verbal legacy, from their poetry and prose writings to their talk, supplemented by a sharp awareness of what contemporaries thought of them. Furthermore, there is always the sense with De Quincey that there is something new and exciting about the poets he has made so integral to his own life and life-writings. His narrative mode is an attempt to communicate his own essence, his core – his *self*. But this self can look disputable. If he has tried, in the Talmudic sense, to 'eat' Wordsworth and Coleridge, it does show. But only up to a point. The picture we have been left with is of the artist more than the sitters (who did not want to be sitters).

It is a cursed picture – it has the curse of secondariness. Self-glamourizing as much as it is self-reviling, this self-portrait continues to be discovered, looked at, and learned from, by readers who, seeing something of themselves in it, delightedly wonder where it has been all their lives. It continues to be treasured with that singular energy a certain kind of reader has for the few books that tell him something of his own story. It continues to be hidden – or half-hidden – in pride and shame behind the curtain in Romanticism's dusty attic.

De Quincey could not free himself from the influence of Wordsworth and Coleridge. Or perhaps it would be more accurate to say that De Quincey never sought to free himself from them. These two founding fathers of English Romanticism seemed to De Quincey to prefigure himself. Their work seemed to him to contain the story of his own life, written before he had lived it.

FURTHER READING

By De Quincey

The Works of Thomas De Quincey, edited by Grevel Lindop, 21 volumes (Pickering and Chatto, London, 2000-2003)

The Collected Writings of Thomas De Quincey, edited by David Masson, 14 volumes (Black, London., 1889-1890)

Confessions of an English Opium-Eater and Other Writings, edited by Robert Morrison (Oxford World Classics, 2013)

Confessions of an English Opium-Eater and Other Writings, edited by Barry Milligan (Penguin Classics, 2003)

Recollections of the Lakes and the Lake Poets, edited by David Wright (Penguin, 1970)

Memorials. Being Letters and Other Records Here First Published, edited by Alexander Japp,2 volumes (John W. Lovell Company, New York, 1891)

A Diary of Thomas De Quincey, 1803, edited by Horace Eaton (N. Douglas, London, 1927)

About De Quincey

Fred Burwick, *Thomas De Quincey: Knowledge and Power* (Palgrave Macmillan UK, 2001)

Albert Goldman, *The Mine and the Mint: Sources For the Writings of Thomas De Quincey* (Southern Illinois University Press, 1965)

Alexander Japp, *Thomas De Quincey: His Life and Writings*, 2 volumes (J. Hogg, London, 1890)

Grevel Lindop, *The Opium-Eater: A Life of Thomas De Quincey* (Taplinger Publishing Company, New York, 1981)

Robert Morrison, *Thomas De Quincey: The English Opium-Eater* (Weidenfeld & Nicolson, 2008)

Edward Sackville-West, *A Flame in Sunlight: Life and Work of Thomas De Quincey* (Cassell, London, 1936)

Nicholas Spice, 'The Animalcule', *London Review of Books*, 18 May 2017

Frances Wilson, *Guilty Thing: A Life of Thomas De Quincey* (Bloomsbury, 2016)

Other Poets

Charles Baudelaire, *The Mirror of Art* (Phaidon Publishers, New York, 1955)

——————————, *The Flowers of Evil*, translated by Anthony Mortimer (Alma Classics Dual language edition, 2016)

——————————, *The Prose Poems and La Fanfarlo*, translated by Rosemary Lloyd (Oxford University Press, 1991)

——————————, *Artificial Paradises* (1860), translated by Stacy Diamond (Kensington, 1994)

William Blake, *Selected Poems* (Oxford World Classics, 2019)

Samuel Taylor Coleridge, *Biographia Literaria*, edited by George Watson (Everyman's Library, 1956)

——————, *Selected Poetry and Prose*, edited by Kathleen Raine (Poetry Library, Penguin, 1957)

——————, *The Notebooks of Samuel Taylor Coleridge*, edited by Kathleen Coburn (Bollingen Series, Princeton, 1957-2002)

——————, *Collected Letters of Samuel Taylor Coleridge*, edited by E.L. Griggs (Oxford University Press, 1956-71)

——————, *The Literary Remains of Samuel Taylor Coleridge*, collected and edited by Henry Nelson Coleridge, volume 1, 1836

John Keats, *The Poetical Works*, edited by H.W. Garrod (Oxford University Press, 1958)

The Poetical Works of Shelley, edited by Newell F. Ford (Houghton Mifflin Company, Boston, 1974)

The Works of Alfred Lord Tennyson (Wordsworth Poetry Library, 1994)

William Wordsworth, The Prelude: Or, Growth of a Poet's Mind (Text of 1805), edited by Ernest De Selincourt and corrected by Stephen Gill (Oxford Standard Authors, 1970)

Other Works Consulted

John Beer, *Coleridge's Play of Mind* (Oxford University Press, 2010)

——————, *Romantic Consciousness: Blake to Mary Shelley* (Palgrave Macmillan, 2003)

Steven George Critchley, 'Pagan Taylor: The Emergence of a Public Character 1785-1804. An Enquiry into the Life and Selected Works of Thomas Taylor the Platonist (1758-1835)' (PhD Thesis, University of York, 2006)

John Danby, *The Simple Wordsworth: Studies in the Poems 1797-1807* (Routledge & Keegan Paul, 1960)

Norman Fruman *Coleridge: The Damaged Archangel* (George Braziller, New York, 1971)

Stephen Gill, *William Wordsworth: A Life* (Oxford University Press, 1990)

William Hazlitt, *Spirit of the Age* (1825), edited by E.D. Mackerness (Plymouth: Northcote House, 1991)

Richard Holmes, *Coleridge: Early Visions* (Hodder and Stoughton, 1989)

H.P. Lovecraft, *The Call of Cthulhu* (Pocket Penguins, 2016)

Seamus Perry, *Tennyson* (Writers and Their Work, Northcote House Publishers Ltd., Devon, 2005)

Plotinus Collected Writings, translated by Thomas Taylor (Prometheus Trust, Somerset, 2000)

Mario Praz, *The Romantic Agony* (Fontana Library, 1933)

Jill Purce, *The Mystic Spiral: Journey of the Soul* (Thames and Hudson, 1974)

Kathleen Raine, *That Wondrous Pattern: Essays on Poetry and Poets* (Counterpoint Press, 2017)

Henry Crabb Robinson, *On Books and Their Authors*, 1, edited by Edith J. Morley (J.M Dent & Sons Limited, London, 1938)

Margaret Russett, *De Quincey's Romanticism: Canonical Minority and the Forms of Transmission* (Cambridge University Press, 2008)

Will Self, *Scale* (Penguin 60s, 1995)

William Shakespeare, *Hamlet* (Penguin Shakespeare, 2005)

Sally Shuttleworth, *The Mind of the Child* (Oxford University Press, 2010)

Alan Vardy, *Constructing Coleridge: The Posthumous Life of the Author.* Basingstoke: Palgrave Macmillan, 2010)

Renŭ Wellek, *Confrontations: Studies in the Intellectual and Literary Relations Between Germany, England and the United States During the Nineteenth Century* (Princeton University Press, 1965)

INDEX